NATIONAL NEW MEDIA ART AWARD 2012

QUEENSLAND ART GALLERY | GALLERY OF MODERN ART

PUBLISHER

Queensland Art Gallery | Gallery of Modern Art
Stanley Place, South Bank, Brisbane
PO Box 3686, South Brisbane
Queensland 4101 Australia
qagoma.qld.gov.au

Published for the 'National New Media Art Award 2012', organised by the Queensland Art Gallery | Gallery of Modern Art and held at the Gallery of Modern Art, 3 August – 4 November 2012.

NATIONAL LIBRARY OF AUSTRALIA CATALOGUING-IN-PUBLICATION DATA:

Title: National New Media Art Award 2012 / Peter McKay; Amanda Slack-Smith.
ISBN: 9781921503450 (pbk.)
Notes: Includes bibliographical references.
Subjects: Art, Australian--21st century--Awards--Queensland.
Art, Australian--21st century--Exhibitions.
Other Authors/Contributors: McKay, Peter. Slack-Smith, Amanda.
Queensland Art Gallery.
Dewey Number: 700.79943

NOTES ON THE PUBLICATION

Dimensions of works are given in centimetres (cm), height preceding width followed by depth. Captions generally appear as supplied.

All photography is credited as known. All images are courtesy the artists, unless otherwise credited.

All artist biographies appear as supplied.

Typeset in Flama. Printed on HannoArt Silk from KW Doggett by Printcraft, Brisbane.

COVER
Robin Fox
CRT: homage to Léon Theremin (details) 2012
Photographs: Nick Roux

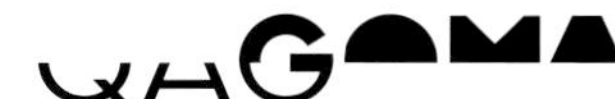

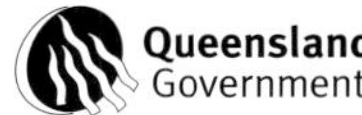

CONTENTS

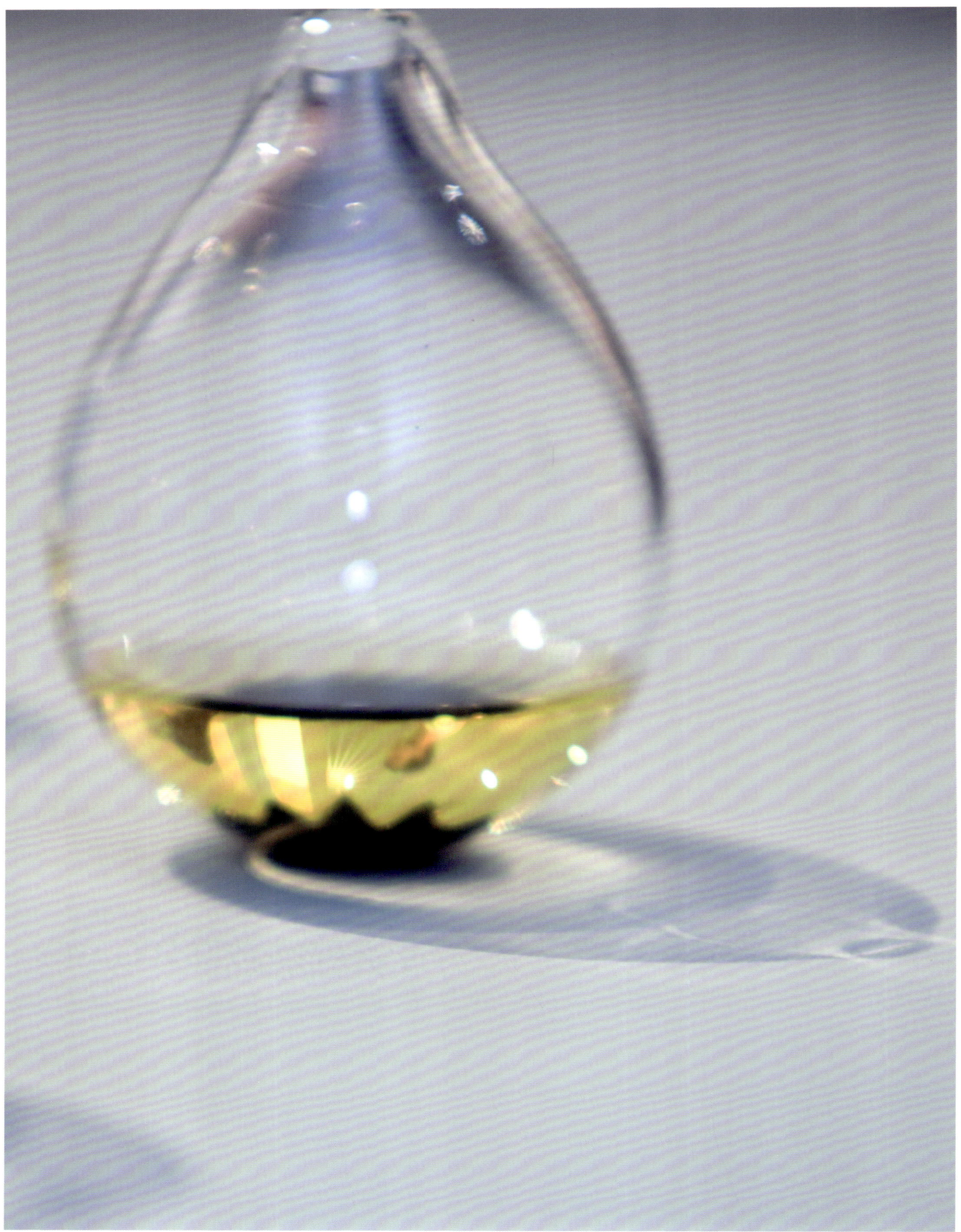

INTRODUCTION

The 'National New Media Art Award 2012' features outstanding works by Australian artists who use technology and new media — including robotics, medical apparatus and motion-controlled musical instruments — to engage with the viewer. Each of these innovative works demonstrates the unique ways artists are adopting new media to comment on contemporary society and culture.

This program, which began in 2008, was conceived as a series of three biennial exhibitions, making this the final instalment. We gratefully acknowledge Campbell Newman, MP, Premier of Queensland, and Ros Bates, MP, Minister for Science, Information Technology, Innovation and the Arts, for supporting this acquisitive Award, as well as the Queensland Government for its commitment to fostering arts, technology and innovation in the state. This program has set a benchmark for supporting the next generation of Australia's new media artists. Similarly, it has made an important assertion about Queensland's commitment to supporting innovation in the visual arts.

I thank everyone who has been involved in the National New Media Art Award for 2012 — particularly the selection committee members Suhanya Raffel, Deputy Director, Curatorial and Collection Development, QAGOMA; Daniel Crooks, new media artist; and Amy Barrett-Lennard, Director, Perth Institute of Contemporary Arts; along with the Gallery's curators Peter McKay, Curator, Contemporary Australian Art, and Amanda Slack-Smith, Assistant Curator, Australian Cinémathèque; and all the Gallery staff involved in the project.

I also congratulate the artists selected for this year's Award exhibition — Kirsty Boyle, Karen Casey, Robin Fox, Ian Haig, Leah Heiss, George Poonkhin Khut, Ross Manning and the collaborative team Petra Gemeinboeck and Rob Saunders — and invite visitors to the Gallery to enjoy these artists' outstanding works.

Tony Ellwood
Director

Leah Heiss
Polarise (detail) 2009
Installation view, fortyfivedownstairs, Melbourne
Photograph: Narelle Sheean

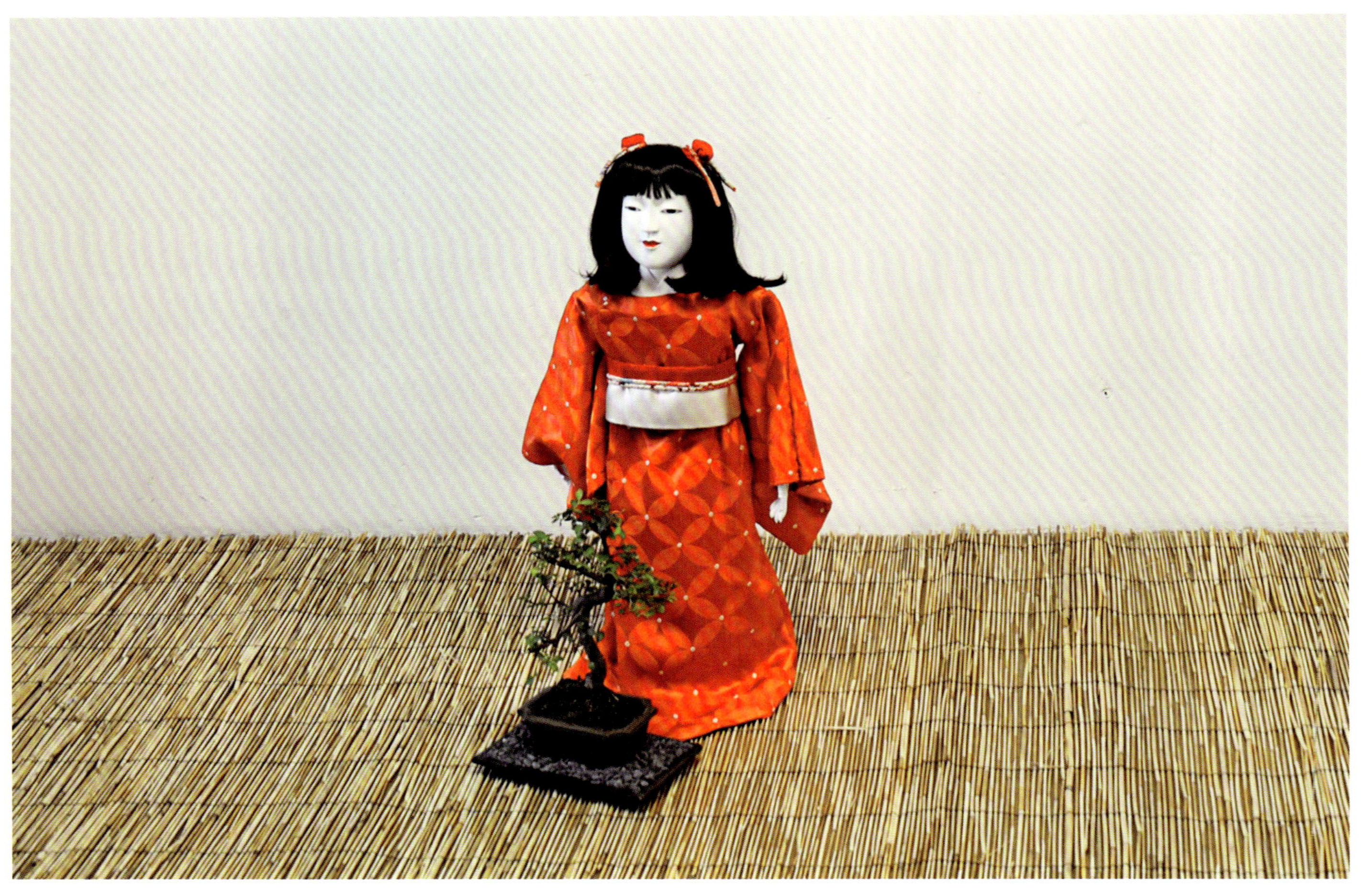

Kirsty Boyle

Performing traditions and technologies

Conjuring ideas of a futuristic realm in which objects perform feats using artificial intelligence, robots capture the imagination. With *Tree ceremony* 2010, Kirsty Boyle explores the intriguing history of robotics, automata and puppetry, developing a performance which combines century-old traditions with innovative, mechanised technologies.

The personification of objects is a human tendency: we project our own image onto inanimate objects, using technology to create new possibilities, striving to recreate human movement. This process raises questions of identity as we experience technology mimicking our actions and navigate the psychology of artificial intelligence. In science fiction films, this process is often presented as a dark scenario — machines perform human actions and destructive human–machine conflicts inevitably arise.

This troubled outlook contrasts with the predominantly benign Japanese view. With its widespread fascination and affection for technology, Japan is considered a world leader in the development of humanoid robots. This allure of 'human technology' has permeated the Japanese cultural psyche, as witnessed in popular culture such as manga and anime, and as embodied by Osamu Tezuka's nationally celebrated hero Astro Boy, created in the 1950s. All these ideas inform Boyle's practice, which explores the evolving history of robotics.

Developed in Japan from early mechanics and automata from eastern Asia, *karakuri* is a mechanical device intended to trick or surprise. When applied to the creation of dolls or puppets, they are known as *karakuri ningyo*. Kirsty Boyle is the sole student of Tamaya Shobei, a ninth-generation and last-surviving master of *karakuri ningyo*, who continues this blend of craft, engineering and performance, creating articulated figures that can perform all kinds of human-like functions and interactions.

The *karakuri* tea-serving doll (*chahakobi*) is considered the first home entertainment robot in Japan, and a forerunner of the more contemporary walking robots now developed by companies like Sony, Toyota and Toshiba. Conveying a magical, spiritual quality (and believed to embody a *kami* or spirit), *karakuri ningyo* are associated with Shintoism,

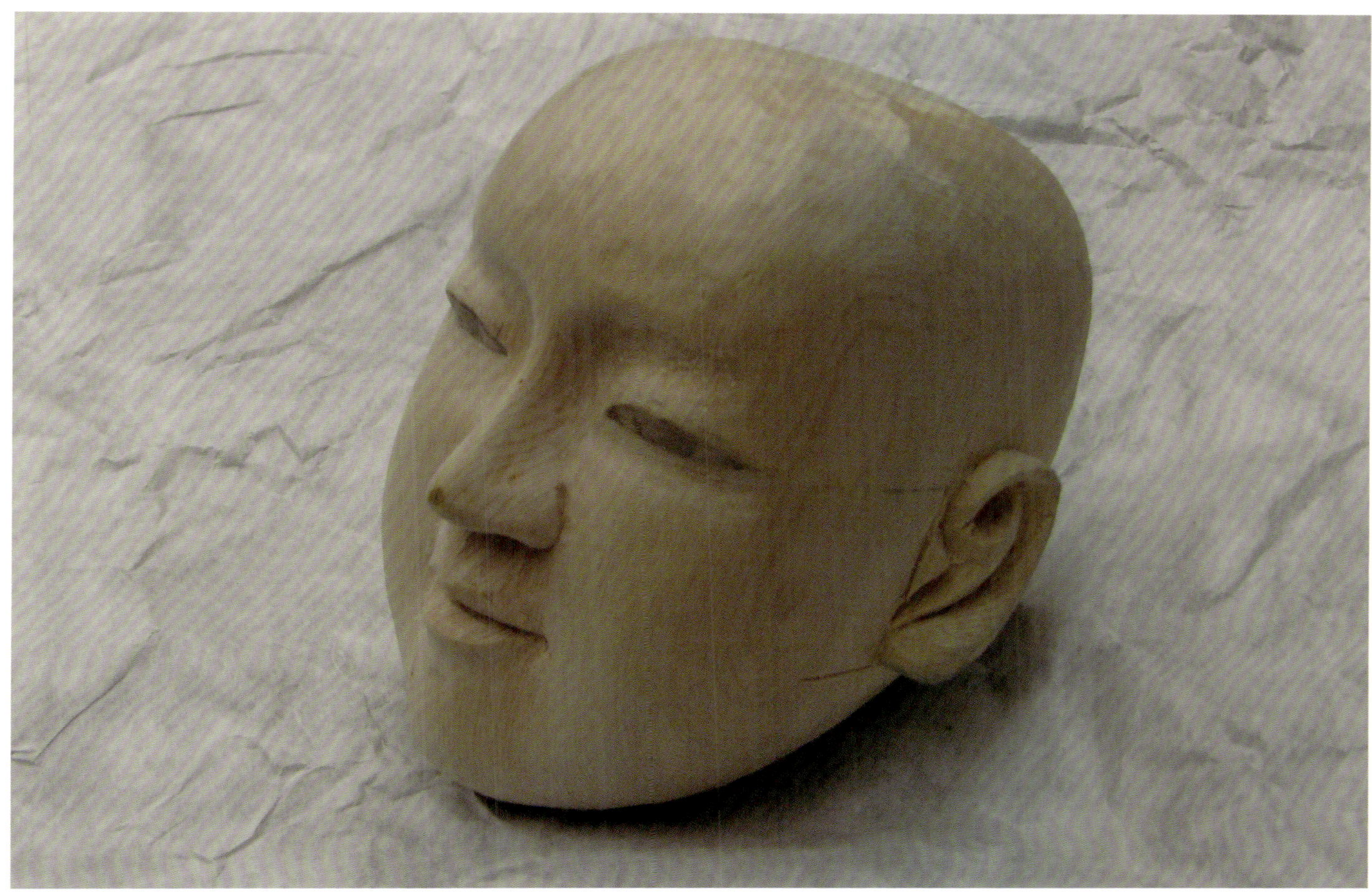

the indigenous religion of Japan. They are celebrated in shrines and as part of festivals, communicating the gestures and sensibilities of traditional theatre and the tea ceremony. By incorporating *karakuri ningyo* into her practice, Boyle has developed a detailed knowledge of Japanese traditions, including techniques of traditional painting, calligraphy, carving, mechanics, costume design and performance.

When Japan opened up to trade with the West in the nineteenth century, some of the greatest technological advances of the time could be found in Swiss-made clocks, which were appropriated by Japanese craftsmen for their mechanical rather than timekeeping functions. In a fortuitous return to this East-West technological exchange, Boyle's experimentations developed into an arts residency at the University of Zurich.[1] By engaging with the evolution of *karakuri* and robotics, Boyle explored the disciplines of digital design and electronic and mechanical engineering, developing a nuanced understanding of robot culture and automata.

Tree ceremony — created by Boyle under her teacher's guidance in Japan, as well as in her Swiss studio — features a kimono-wearing *karakuri ningyo* called Suki, the solo performer. Suki executes a timely and musical combination of movements on stage alongside a bonsai — a juxtaposition of the natural and the animated, referencing the Shinto worship of nature. The work is peaceful and rhythmic, performed to a specially-commissioned musical composition. Evoking the careful gestures of the Japanese tea ceremony and the precise choreography of traditional Japanese theatre, it entices audiences to interact with this humanoid robot.

Integrating the valued element of surprise, Suki magically reveals a mask in her hands and, like a *Noh* theatre actor, constructs a new persona. This gesture signals the underlying premise of Boyle's work, as the mask of a futuristic robot covers Suki's handpainted and carved, cypress wood face.

Kirsty Boyle's *Tree ceremony* presents a unique combination of traditional techniques and new media. The work incorporates fascinating elements and investigates the evolution and philosophical underpinnings of an influential traditional craft and its interactions with technology. Boyle emphasises the value of *karakuri* and the cumulative learning characterising the discipline. Her actions contrast sharply with our conditioned acceptance of the redundancy of continual technology advances, and her work positions innovative thinking combined with hybrid technology as another option for our future.

Tarun Nagesh

Endnote

1 With access to advanced digital technology, Boyle created this *karakuri ningyo*-inspired performance in 2010 under commission from the Museum Tinguely, Basel, and the Kunsthaus Graz, Austria.

Tree ceremony 2010
Work in development, 2010
Photograph (left): Miro Bertozzi

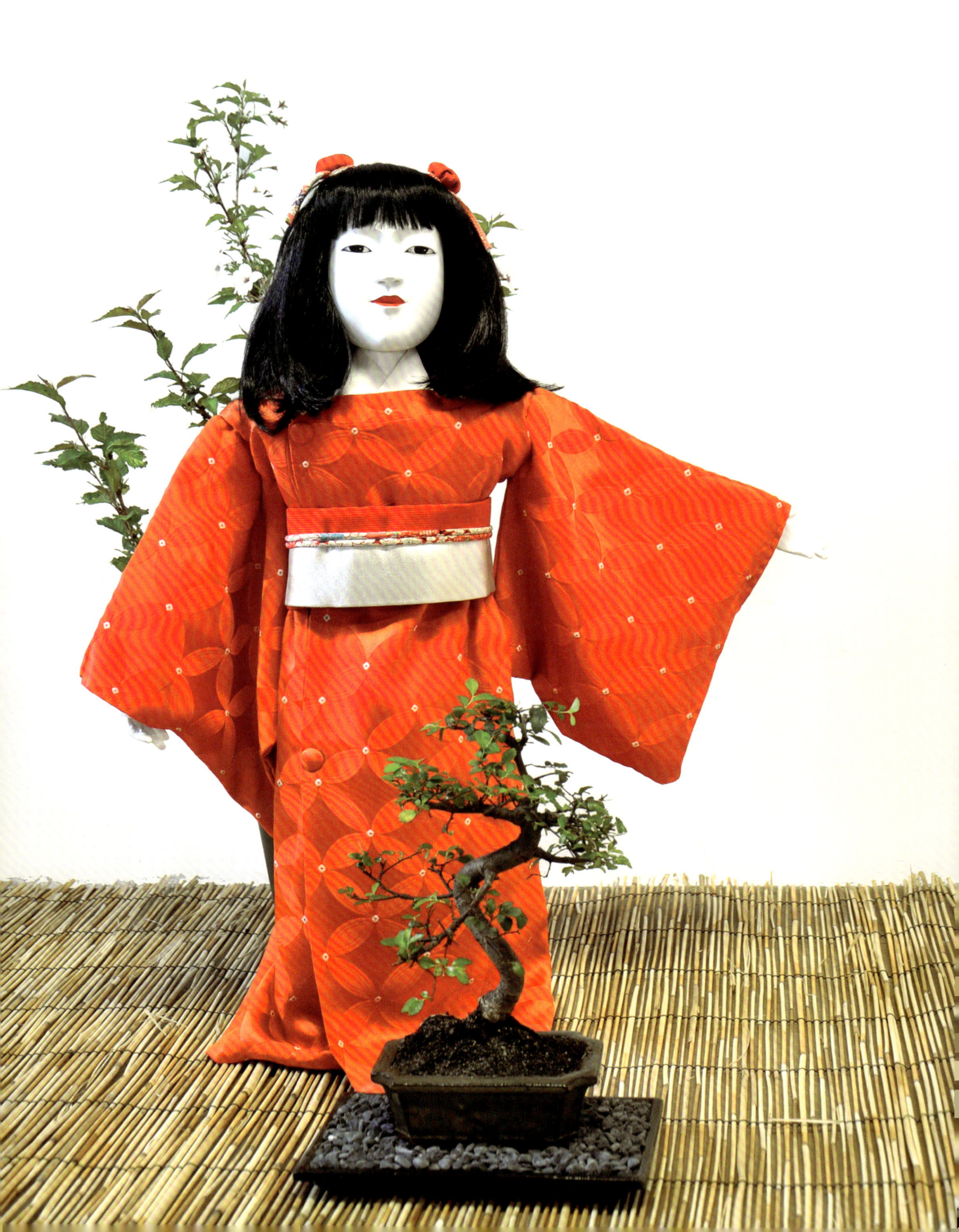

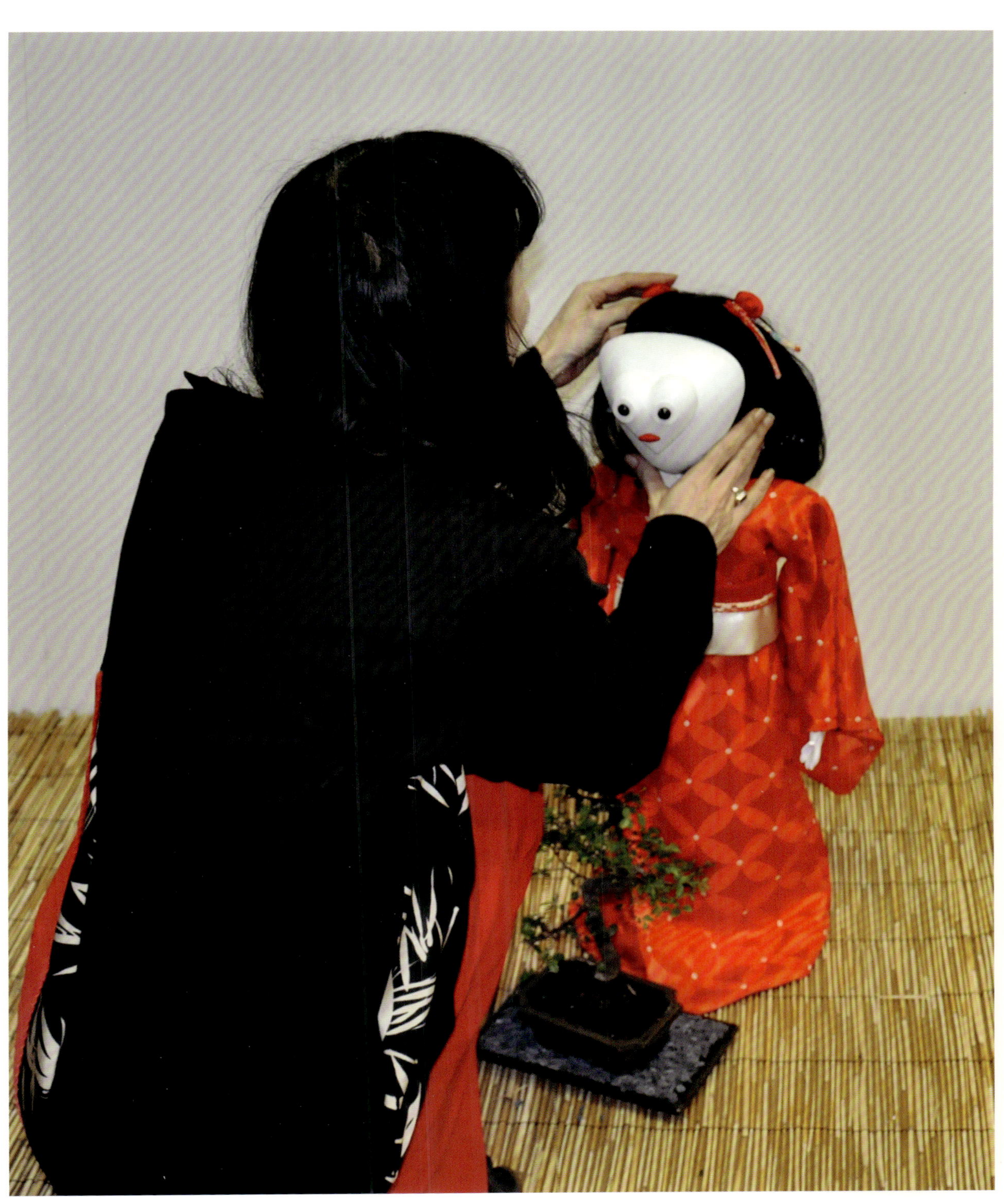

Tree ceremony 2010
Work in development, 2010
Photographs: Miro Bertozzi

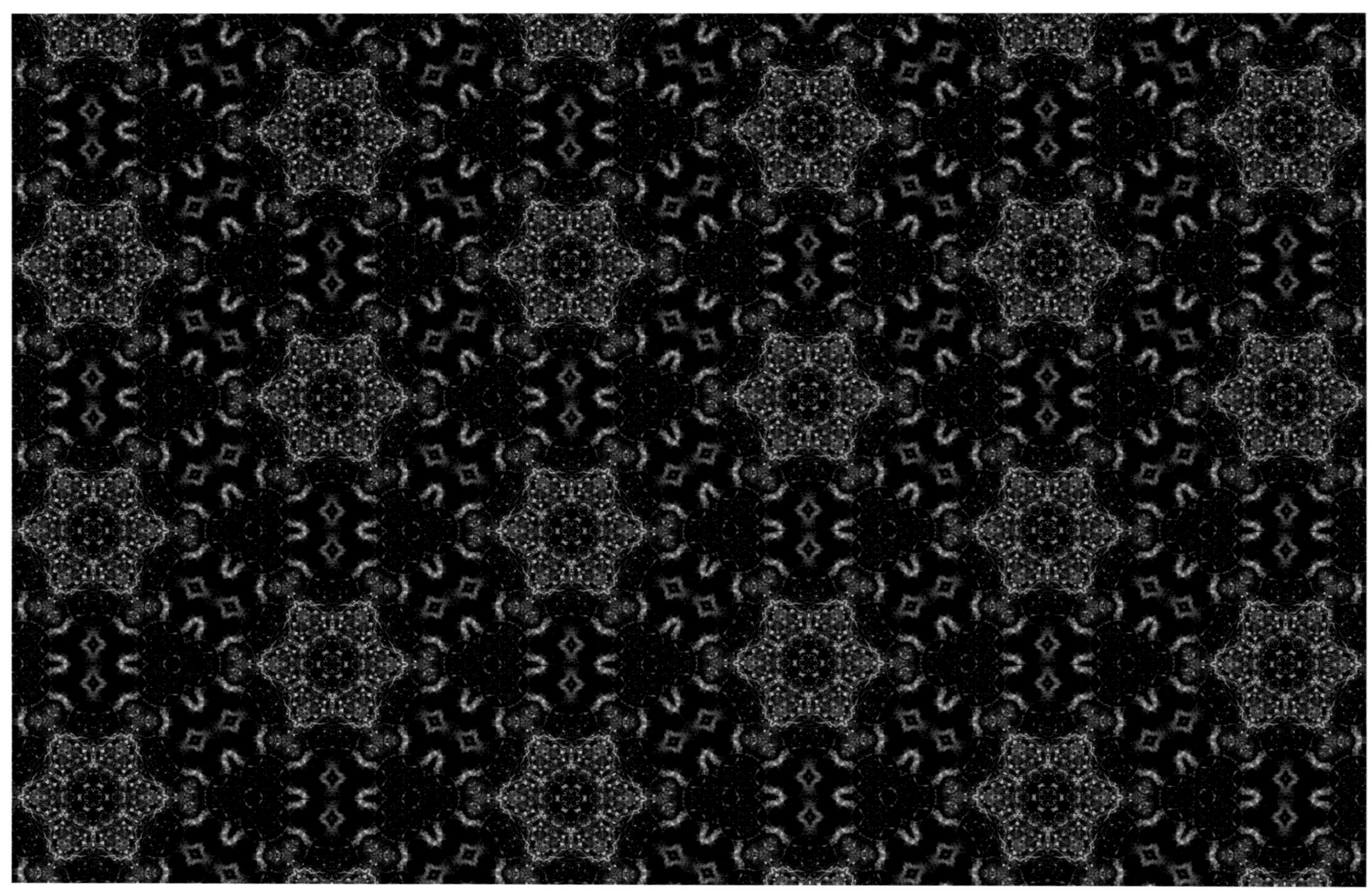

Karen Casey

The art of dreaming: Art of mind

Karen Casey pushes art's technological limits, questioning what happens if the need for mechanical processes is eliminated and if, instead, we simply allow our thoughts to manifest themselves. Through her projections, performances and immersive installations, Casey seeks to alter the states of mind of her audience.

Since 2004, when she first approached the Brain Sciences Institute at Swinburne University, Melbourne, Casey has been working with the recordings of the electrical signals emanating from her own brain. Captured using electroencephalography (commonly known as EEG), these recordings have been the basis for the artist's ongoing inquiry into the mind and creativity. With this aim, Casey approached software developer Harry Sokol to develop VisEEG, a unique program that audiovisually renders neural data in real time.

Over many years, Casey's work has revolved around an ideology of social cohesion, exploring the interconnections of art, science and society, as well as the potential of artistic collaboration. Envisioning a new frontier for art, the artist contemplates establishing an online zone where people can interact using their brainwaves — each person would be linked by means of a portable, commercially-available EEG device — connecting their thoughts in digital space.

Casey used her prerecorded alpha brainwaves as the basis for *Meditation wall* 2011. Of the brainwave frequencies, alpha waves induce a relaxed and meditative mind state, as opposed to the alert beta state or the deep sleep state of delta waves. Originally exhibited as part of the 17th International Symposium of Electronic Art at Istanbul's Sabanci University[1] — and as Casey often explores ideas of place and space, or a merging of cultures and ideas — her kaleidoscopic projection resembled Islamic tiles, morphing from azure hues to the colours of the Australian landscape.[2] This is Casey's way of linking her work to the people, culture or environment in which it is presented. In *Meditation wall*, Casey reflects on the architecture defining Istanbul, and focuses on creating a deeply contemplative space, so important to the daily rituals of the city's inhabitants.

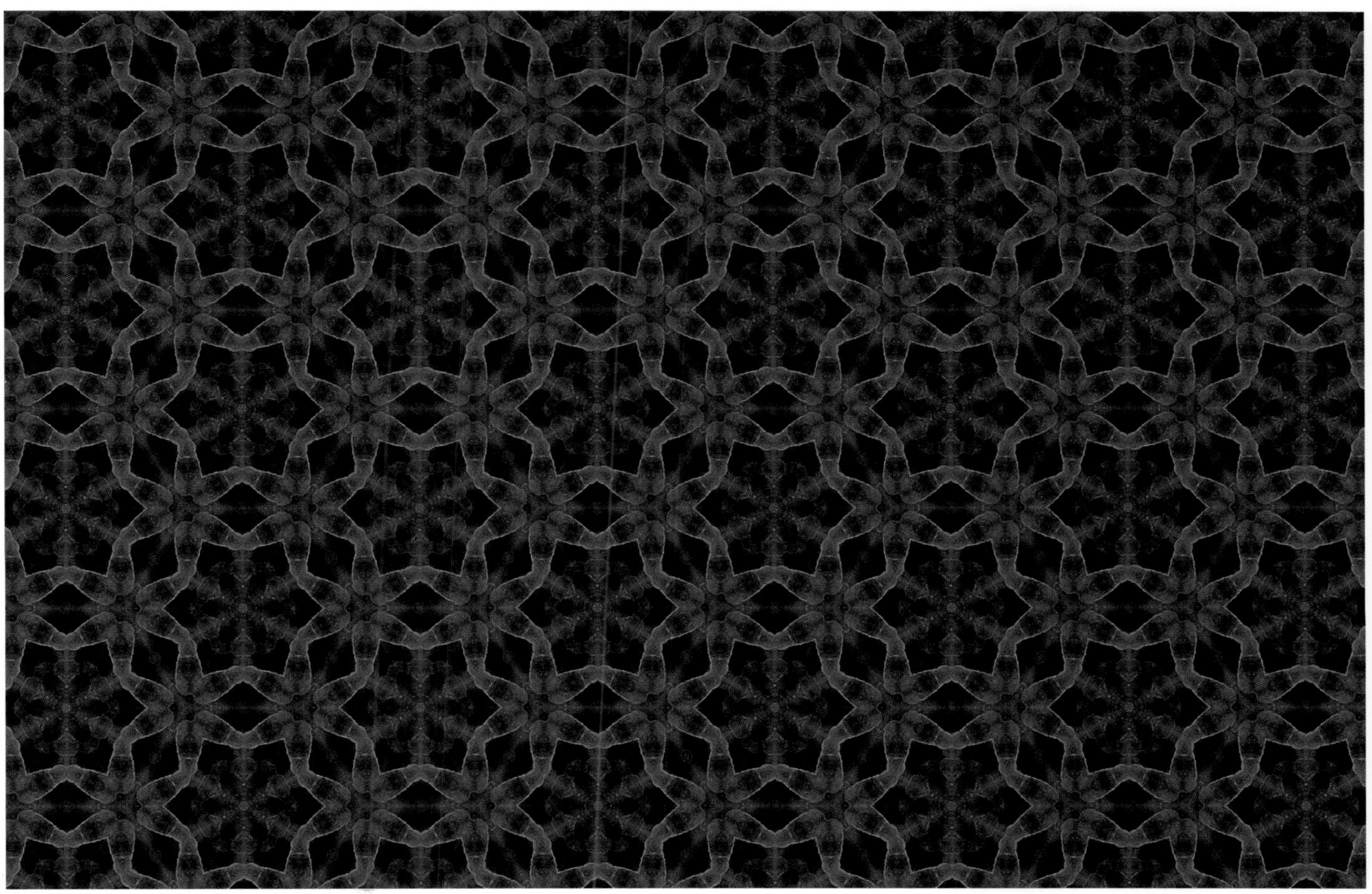

Dream zone (production stills, details) 2012

In *Dream zone* 2012, Casey again establishes this link with place and space, which she privileges through her engagement with the physical parameters of the room, in order to create a changing array of crystalline-shaped patterns.[3] She draws on both her own theta brainwaves, the frequency predominantly associated with dreaming, as well as moments of idle imagination and creative inspiration. Casey's 'dreaming' brainwaves work with the program designed in collaboration with Sokol. The result is an immersive space of ever-changing imagery projected onto the walls. An aural landscape of atmospheric sound is also generated, reflecting the undulating rhythms of the mind. These cerebral waves were in turn recorded in a neuro-feedback process — the artist was simultaneously generating and experiencing the work firsthand.

This transformative meditative experience shares an association with Indigenous ceremony and the dreaming, the spiritual world that coexists with the physical world in which we live. The dreaming is the Aboriginal 'otherplace', a spirit world where the deeds undertaken by ancestral spirits left their permanent mark on our physical world. In our world, these spirits still exist and their deeds still resonate: the dreaming is everywhere and 'everywhen', encompassing the spiritual essence of everything — past, present and future.[4]

As a contemporary artist in an increasingly secular world, Karen Casey does not look to recreate or re-establish a connection to the dreaming, rather, she attempts to elicit a state of mind and create a space where rational thought is disabled, where the theta state is elevated and where creative thought proliferates. She is searching for a pure state of creative being, a space of sublime transcendence. Herein lies the paradox in Casey's practice: she laments the division and separation of the spiritual, the physical and the social in our everyday lives. Yet, through the use of some of the most advanced technological processes, she seeks to return to an exploration of these connections in her art.[5] The artist asks: in our contemporary world, is the use of technology the only way we can connect with a more purely transcendent state of mind?

Bruce McLean

Endnotes

1 *Meditation wall* 2011 was exhibited as part of 'Uncontainable', Cumhuriyet Art Gallery, Istanbul, 2011.
2 Karen Casey, telephone conversation with the author, 25 May 2012.
3 Casey, telephone conversation.
4 In 1968, the anthropologist Professor WEH Stanner presented the Boyer Lectures. In 'After the Dreaming', he used the term 'everywhen' to describe the dreaming, a pre-existing term, though limited in use, meaning 'not fixed in time' or 'of all times, collectively'. It has since become common in describing time in relation to the concept of the dreaming. See Donald McDonald (ed.), *The Boyer Collection: Highlights of the Boyer Lectures 1959–2000*, ABC Books, Sydney, 2001.
5 Artist statement, *The Third Asia Pacific Triennial of Contemporary Art*, Queensland Art Gallery, Brisbane, 1999, see <http://visualarts.qld.gov.au/apt3/artists/artist_bios/karen_casey_a.htm >, viewed 27 May 2012.

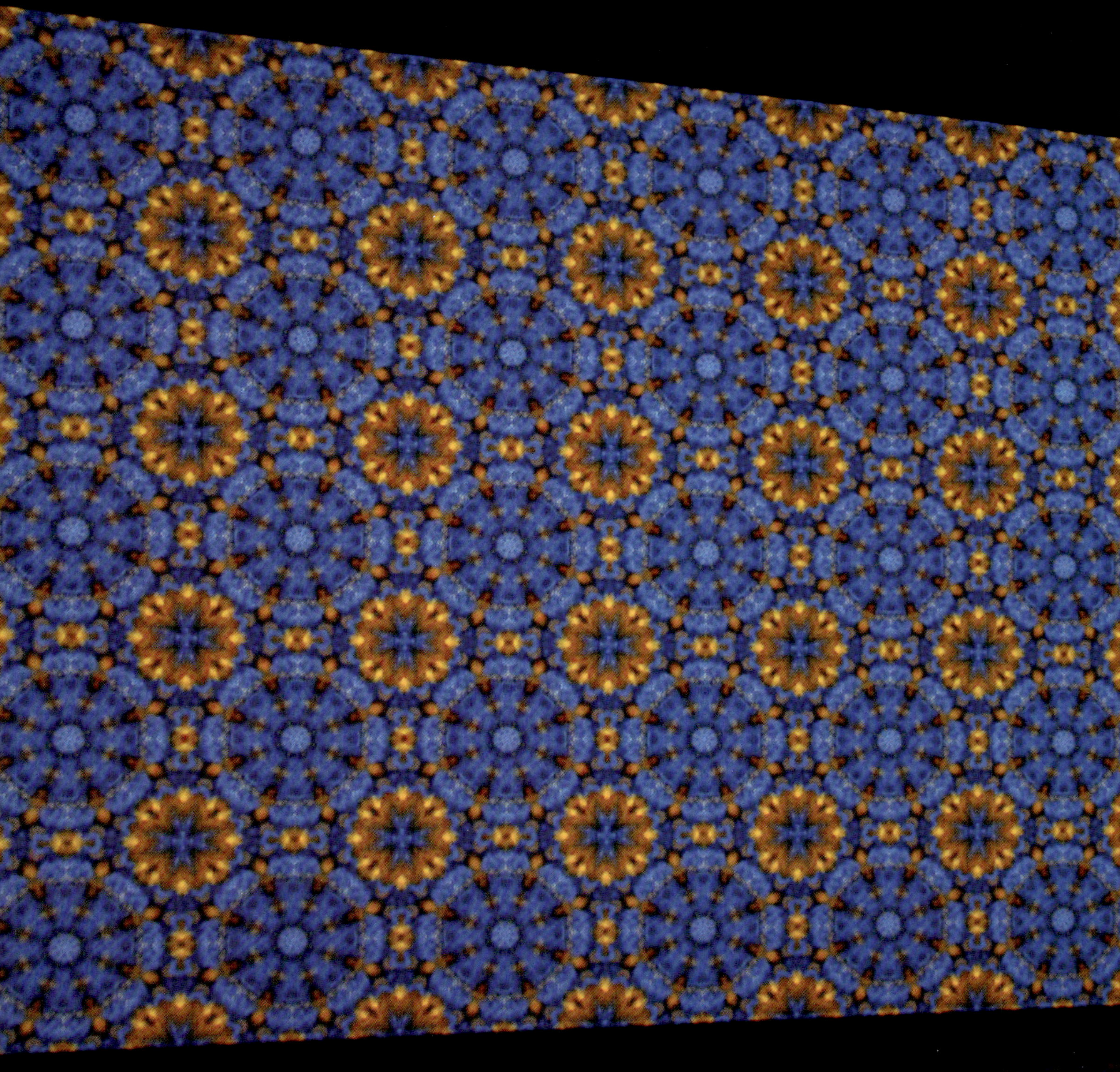

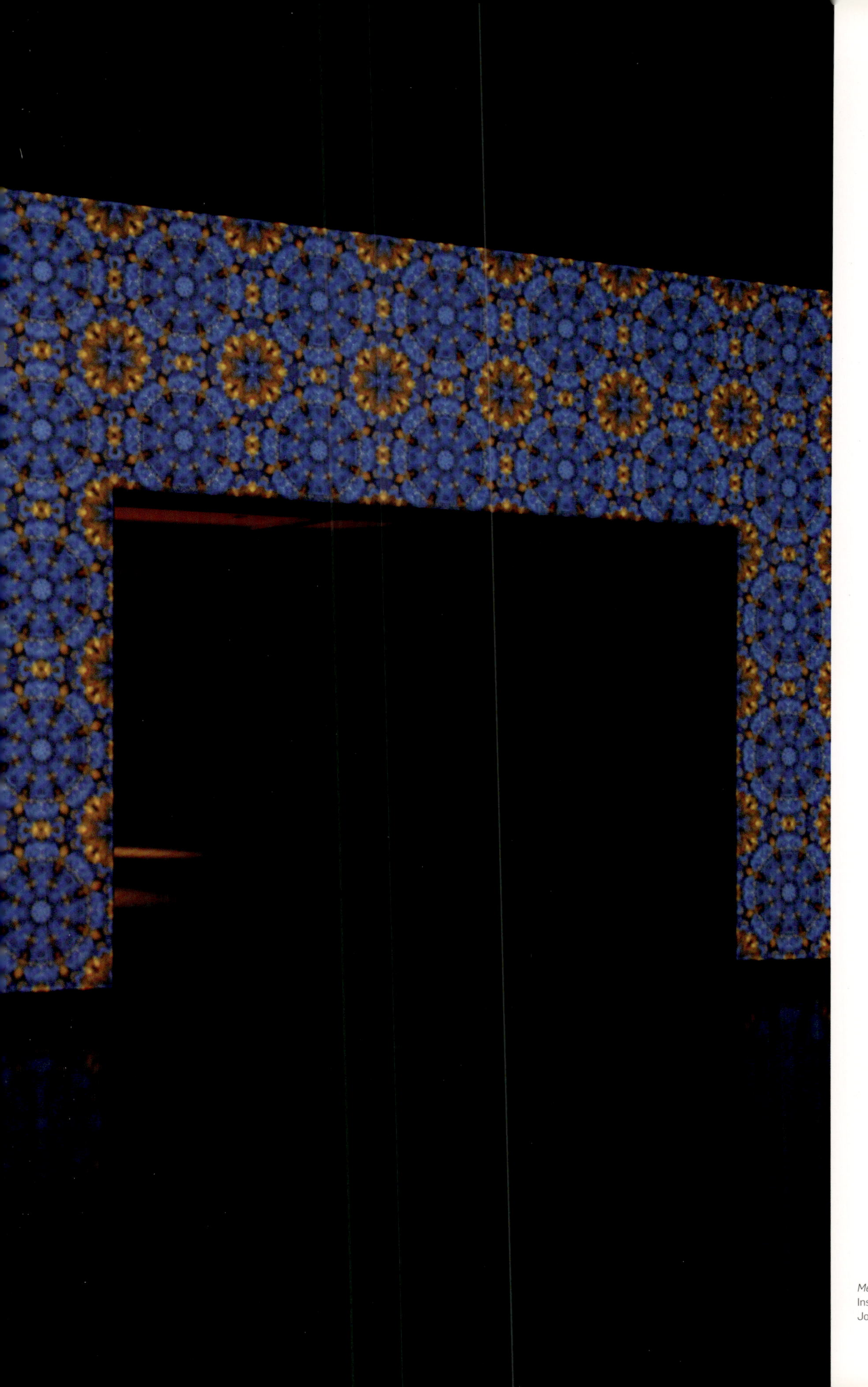

Meditation wall 2011
Installation view,
John Curtin Gallery, Perth, 2012

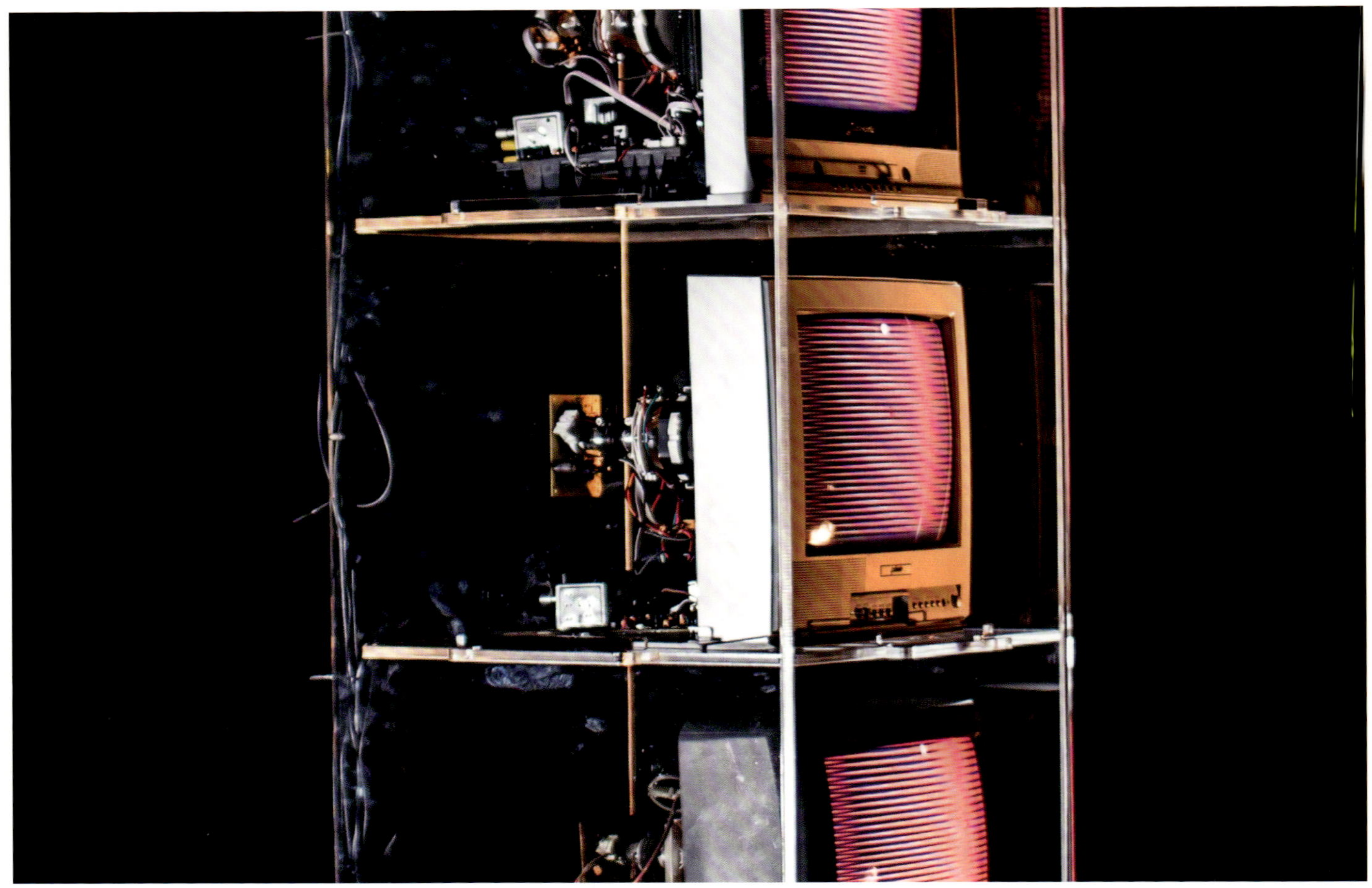

Robin Fox

Between light and sound

The awe of witnessing man's first step on the moon, via the family television set in 1969, has given way to everyday debates about image quality, screen size, internet capability and 3-D technology. Once the epitome of human ingenuity, CRT (cathode-ray tube) televisions are no longer considered magical. Relics of another time, CRT television sets are now discarded, their lead-glass screens found face down in the grass on suburban nature strips, alongside broken chairs and prams — an obsolete technology superseded by style and gadgetry.

For Robin Fox, the abundance of these discarded CRT televisions offers an opportunity to continue investigations into Russian physicist Lev Sergeyevich Termen's 1920s and 1930s experiments in sound and vision. Better known as Léon Theremin, this flamboyant inventor not only developed one of the earliest television devices — a mirror drum-based system interlacing images to achieve a high resolution — he was also an early progenitor of electronic music through his invention of the musical instrument bearing his name, the theremin.[1] Originally developed as a proximity detector for the Russian government, this hands-free instrument's distinctive sound was controlled by the body's movement in relation to two antennae. The eerie beauty of its unique sound captivated audiences and resulted in regular appearances in the soundtracks of North American science fiction films of the 1950s.

In *CRT: homage to Léon Theremin* 2012, Fox combines the ethereal, remote agency of the theremin with the lurid and instantly responsive colour fields of old CRT televisions to create a highly sensitive, interactive audiovisual installation. Stripped of their outer casings, 15 televisions are arranged in three columns and encased in perspex. Each column of televisions receives a direct sound that is sent to the yoke of each television's red, green and blue colour fields, determining the displacement of colour on screen. Combined with multichannel, sound-responsive software and custom-designed motion tracking, this connectivity between sound and light transforms real-time human motion into a celebration of interaction and play. Viewers experience a direct response to the electrical signals created by their movement, resulting in a synaesthetic relationship between movement, sound and light.[2] Fox explains:

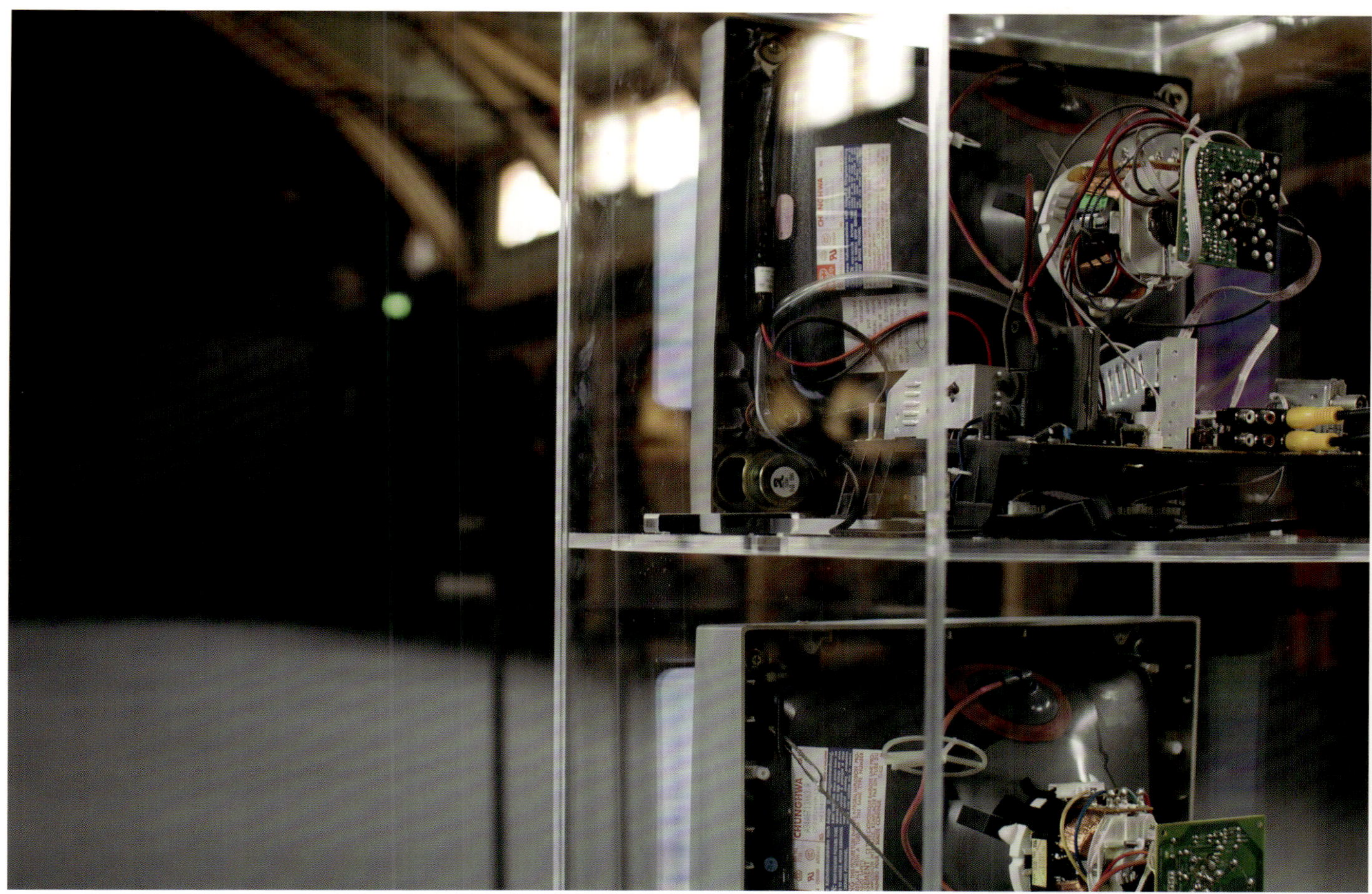

CRT: homage to Léon Theremin (detail) 2012

Left: installation view

Right: work in development, 2012

Photographs: Nick Roux

> Inside each television is a beautiful electromagnetic creation. The tubes themselves use electromagnets to drag individual beams of red, green and blue light at impossible speeds across a phosphorous screen (a screen that has a very short memory, a screen that leaves a momentary trace). The viewer, through movement, controls the screen. The kinetic energy of gesture, real human action, is transformed using cutting-edge technologies into the interplay of sound and light. The television is familiar — it is a trope — and we all know what a television is and what a television means. It is this assumed knowledge that makes the paradigm shift of controlling the television's content interesting.[3]

This seamless integration of old and new media invites up to six people to interact with the work at any one time. Each column tracks two viewers independently through a hidden camera, translating their movements into light and sound. This allows for each column to be 'played' separately, encouraging the audience to create solo or ensemble compositions through a melodic piano scale response. 'Musicians' can alter the pitch and flickering displacement of colour on the screens by modifying the range and speed of their movements, as well as the volume through their proximity to the column of televisions.

For Fox, this integration of performance and communal interaction changes the viewers' preconceived relationship with the television, one characterised by passive consumption, by reversing the flow of information. The ability of audiences to compose their own works, and combine their movements with others to create ensemble compositions, disrupts the perception of screen-based entertainment as an isolating experience that distances viewers from each other. In fact, the televisions lie dormant in Fox's work, and are activated only when engaged by the viewer.

Through *CRT: homage to Léon Theremin,* Robin Fox transforms a purportedly obsolete technology into the catalyst for a vibrant, interactive, electro-acoustic experience that explores the dynamics of performer, space and technology. The work continues the artist's ongoing investigations into multichannel performance on both analog and digital platforms. Here, Fox offers the audience a platform to experience sound and light in a way that mimics the neurological phenomenon of synaethesia. By engaging two or more of the body's senses simultaneously, the audience experiences what they are hearing as what they are seeing.

Amanda Slack-Smith

Endnotes

1 Albert Glinsky, *Theremin: Ether Music and Espionage*, University of Illinois Press, Urbana, Illinois, 2000.
2 Robin Fox, email correspondence with the author, 5 January 2012.
3 Fox, email correspondence.

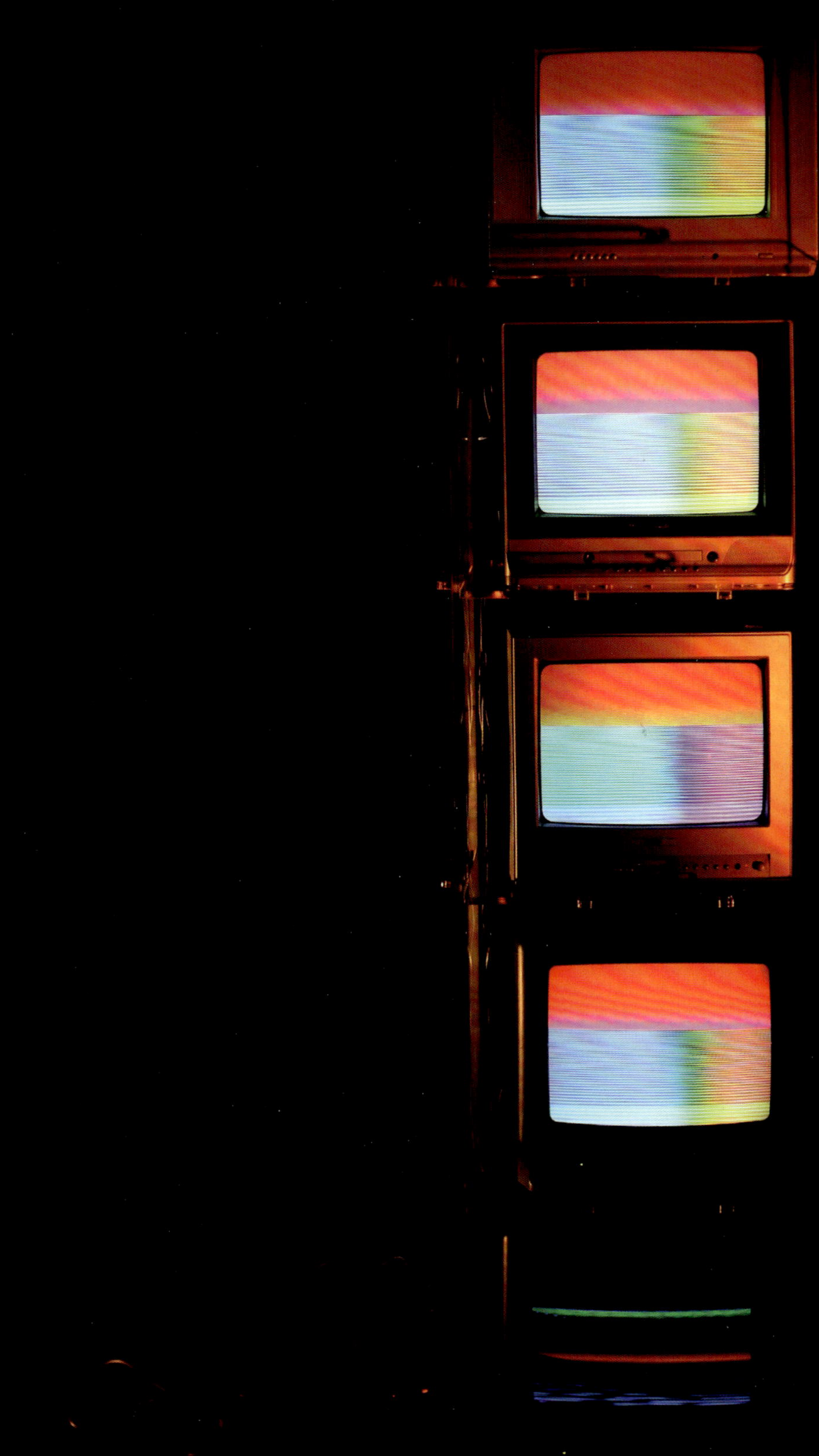

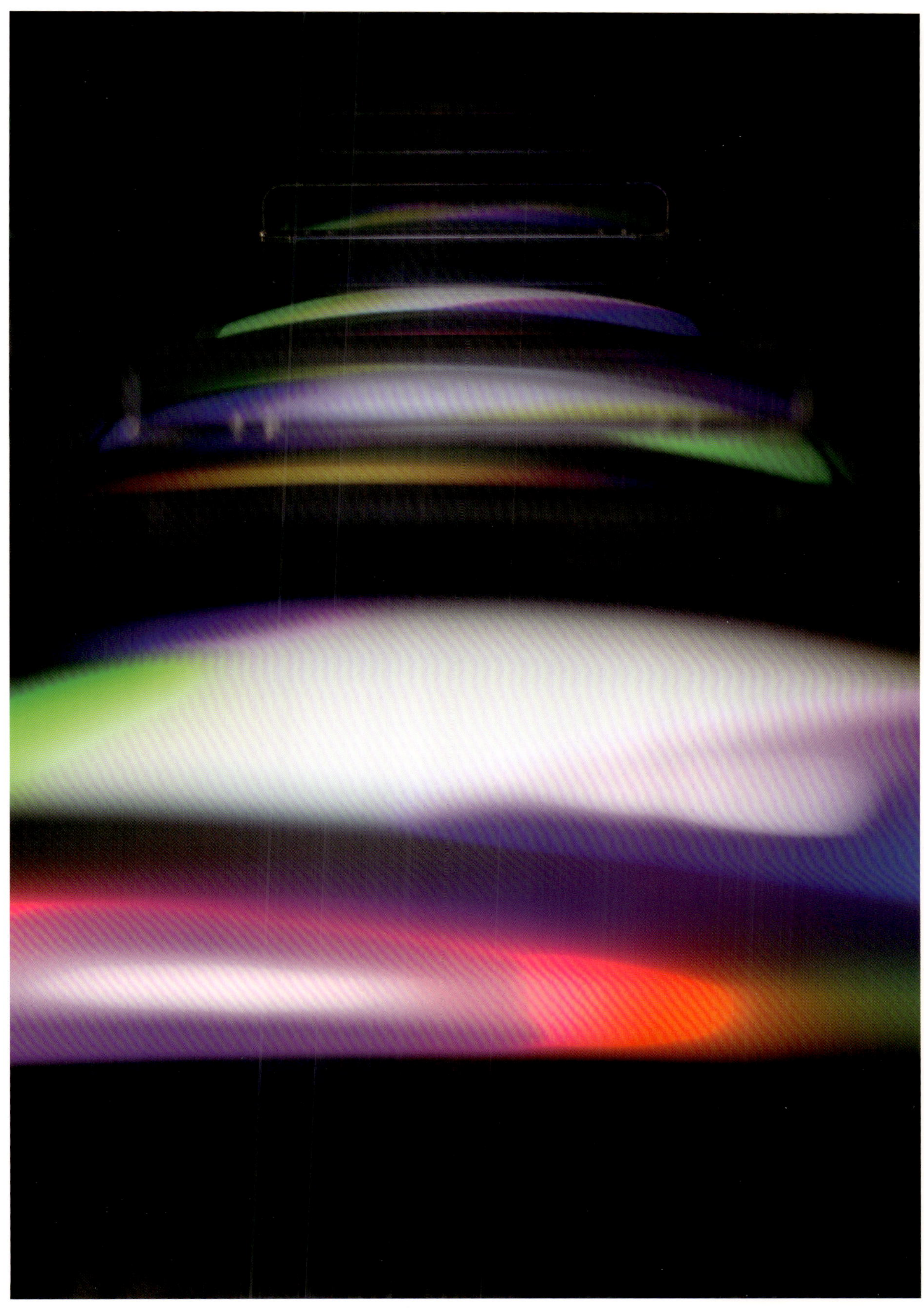

Above: *CRT: homage to Léon Theremin* (detail) 2012
Photograph: Nick Roux
Opposite: *CRT: homage to Léon Theremin* (detail) 2012

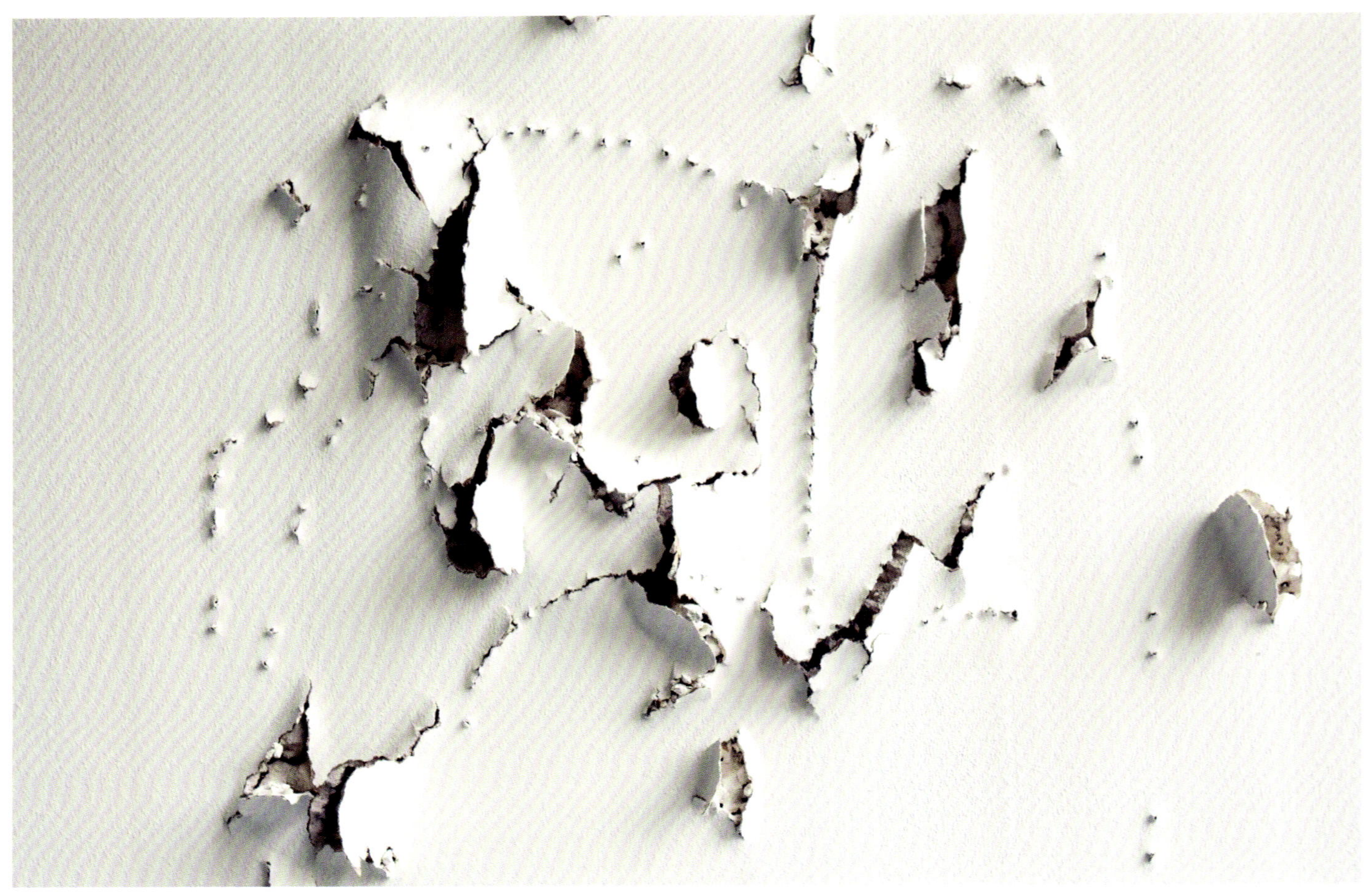

Petra Gemeinboeck and Rob Saunders

The space in between

Technology shapes our behaviour: Petra Gemeinboeck and Rob Saunders understand this interaction more deeply than most. Together, they explore the influence technology has on our lives. As a result, they have recognised a major change: increasingly, the tools we use are no longer simply extensions of ourselves, as German philosopher Martin Heidegger once proposed. In the twenty-first century, we have begun to enrich the technologies we create, which, in the future, might prompt a role reversal — as humans, we might one day become extensions of our robot superiors, should they find us useful enough.

Gemeinboeck and Saunders's specific interest is artificial intelligence, or AI, and the potential for creative agency within machine learning. Their work *Zwischenräume* 2010–12 provides an insight into our present understanding of our place in a future world — a challenge for many, especially when the future involves great change. Exploring this idea, *Zwischenräume* — which translates as 'the space in between' — implants advanced robots, with the capacity to study their environment and respond to it, into the walls of the gallery space. These robots possess AI, so it is not only the audience that interacts with, and contemplates, the work — the capacity for interaction and contemplation is also experienced *by* the work.

When left to their own devices, the robots break through their plasterboard confines, perforating the walls with a series of small holes through which they can see using camera vision. If an 'audience' is present, the robots watch the human onlookers, tracking colour, movement and individual faces in order to enhance their knowledge and alleviate their own programmed 'boredom'. Occasionally, the robots communicate with each other, signalling requests to organise their behaviour and work together. This demonstration of autonomy emulates a degree of consciousness and their presence poses questions — are we on the threshold of an awakening of technology? What will the machines do when they stir?

American inventor and futurist Ray Kurzweil has explored the pace of technological development in depth and has reported on consistent measures showing that innovation falls into a pattern of exponential growth, or what he terms the 'law of accelerating returns', and that dramatic changes might be closer than we realise.[1] Taking history as a guide, Kurzweil suggests the world we inhabit will swiftly become unrecognisable following

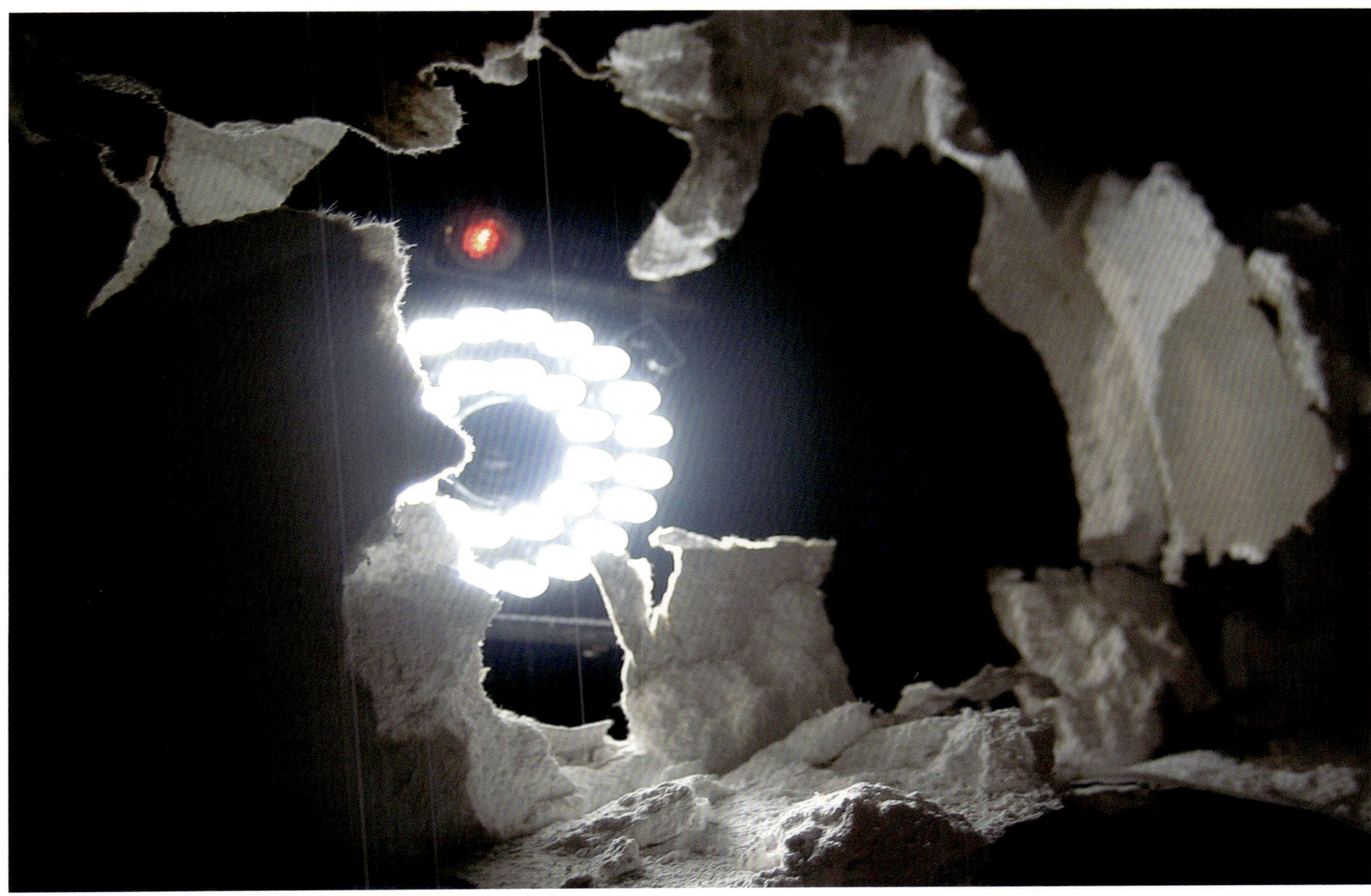

Zwischenräume (details) 2010–12
Installation views, Forum Stadtpark, Graz, Austria, 2011

the creation of an ultra-intelligent machine, with an artificial intelligence greater than our own — particularly one which can merge with our own biology. As he proposes:

> What would 1,000 scientists, each 1,000 times more intelligent than human scientists today, and each operating at 1,000 times faster than contemporary humans (because the information processing in their primarily nonbiological brains is faster) accomplish? One chronological year would be like a millennium for them . . . They would change their own thought processes to enable them to think even faster. When scientists become a million times more intelligent and operate a million times faster, an hour would result in a century of progress (in today's terms).[2]

Kurzweil's vision is grandly optimistic, culminating in a kind of awakening of the universe in which matter itself becomes cognisant and intelligence spreads outwards from the planet Earth. But others question the assumption that ultra-intelligent beings would view us kindly. Why should they? Are humans really as valuable to the cosmos as we believe? Might our innovations inadvertently manifest our own redundancy? Could we be rendered extinct by both the depth and limitations of our own intelligence? Theorist Eliezer Yudkowsky argues that the past is no point from which to accurately predict the future, that our steps forward demand caution — and that our success can be accompanied by unintended outcomes. To those working in fields with the potential for unforeseen ramifications, Yudkowsky warns:

> Someone should remember the history of errors in physics calculations: the Castle Bravo nuclear test that produced a 15-megaton explosion, instead of a 4 to 8, because of an unconsidered reaction in lithium-7: they correctly solved the wrong equation, failed to think of all the terms that needed to be included, and at least one person in the expanded fallout radius died.[3]

Tethered to the space they occupy, Petra Gemeinboeck and Rob Saunders's lurking robots pose little threat, although they are 'networked'. Their animation enriches our concepts of hybridisation and stimulates our concepts of a future cultural, social and political landscape that will be shared with cognisant machines. Though this discussion reads like science fiction, such a trajectory is surprisingly conceivable. Whether they be friend or foe, future generations of curious robots will undoubtedly enjoy greater freedom than Gemeinboeck and Saunders's do. While there is a question as to who should develop, own and control such technology, perhaps the more substantial concern will be: how will the freedom and autonomy granted to future robots eventually affect our own?

Peter McKay

Endnotes

1 Ray Kurzweil, *The Singularity is Near: When Humans Transcend Biology*, Duckworth Overlook, London [Kindle edition], 2008, location 1069 of 18238.
2 Kurzweil, location 798 of 18238.
3 Eliezer Yudkowsky, quoted in Nick Bostrom and Milan M Ćirković (eds.), 'Cognitive biases potentially affecting judgment of global risks', in *Global Catastrophic Risks*, Oxford University Press, Oxford [Kindle edition], 2008, location 2815 of 13592.

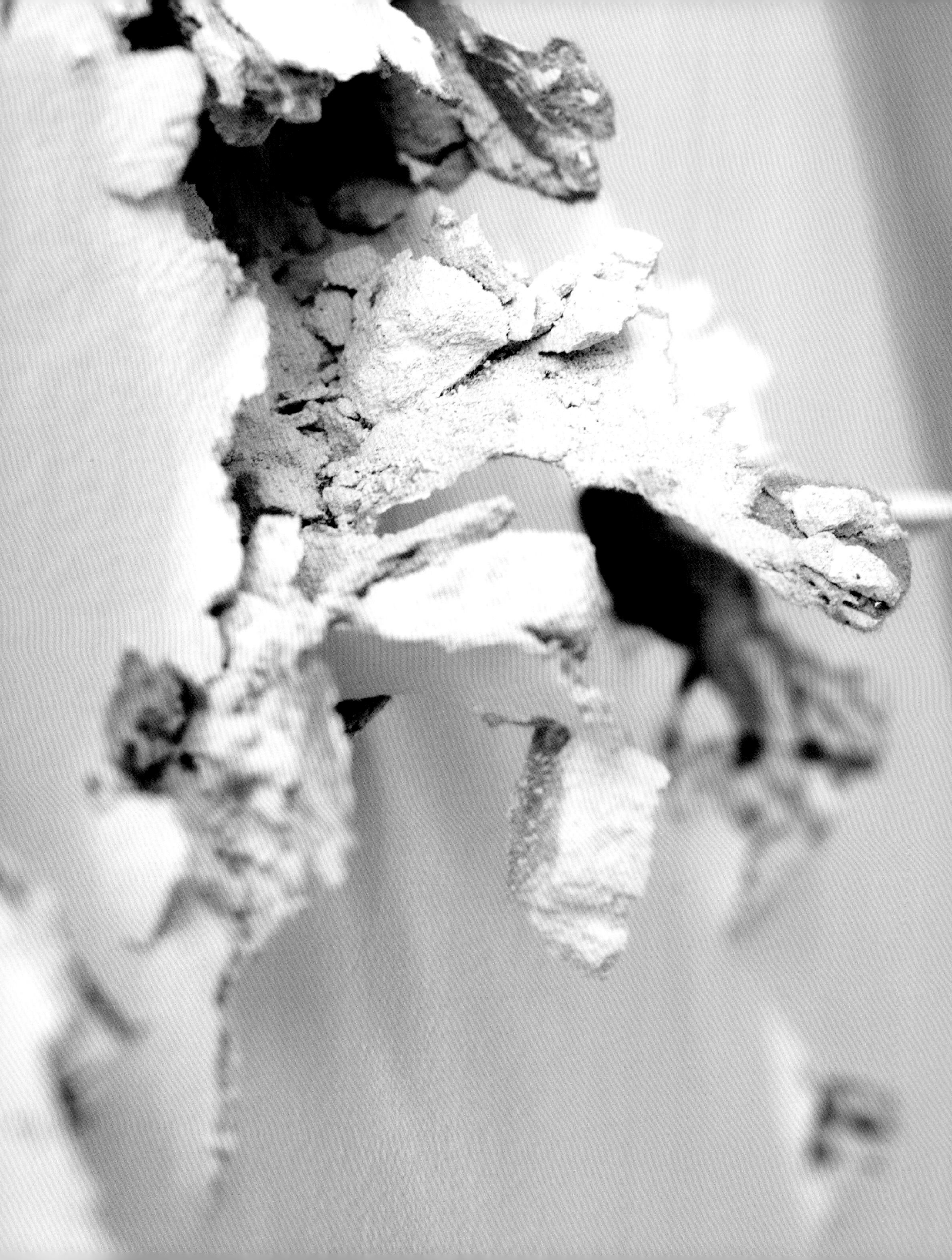

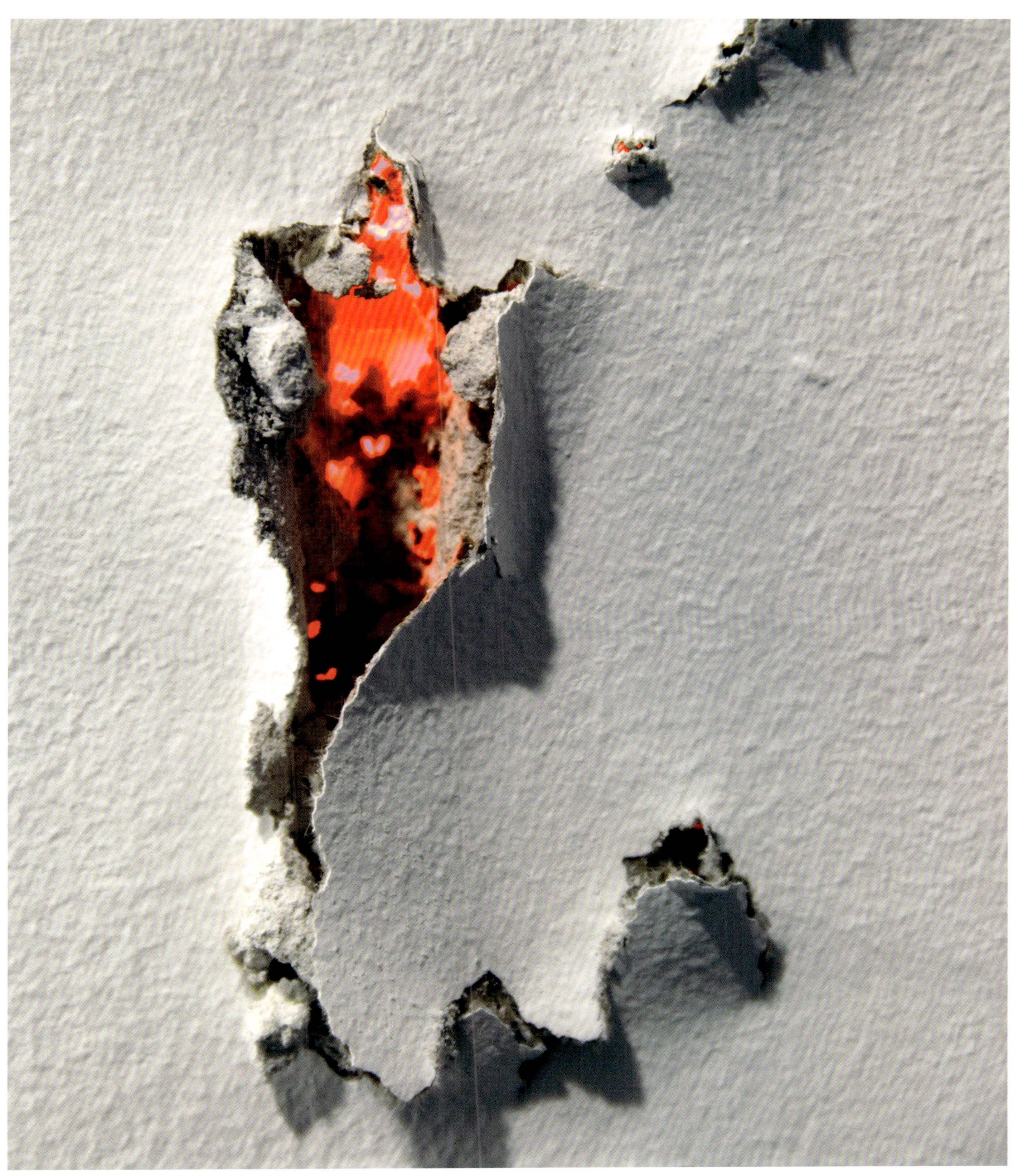

Zwischenräume (details) 2010–12

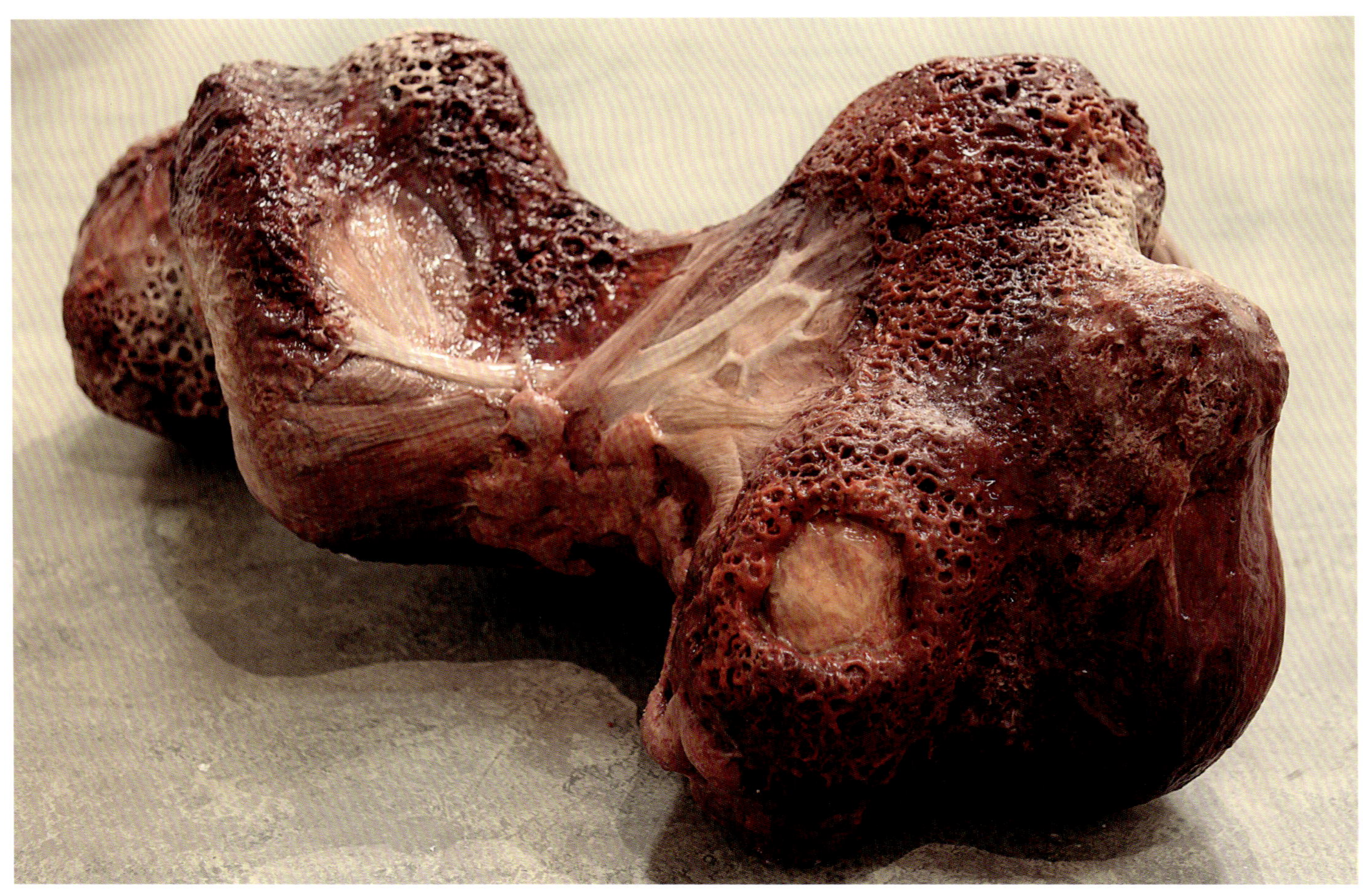

Ian Haig

It came from within

Ian Haig investigates alternate visions of the everyday, combining popular culture influences with an uncanny understanding of the absurd. Much of Haig's work focuses on the internal mechanics of the human body, exploring themes of transformation and a variety of psychopathological states. Haig realises this through the investigation of ideas of attraction and repulsion involving flesh, fluids and bodily functions. Both playful and provoking, Haig's works offer astute critiques of the societal discomfort surrounding the less palatable realities of the human condition — namely, ageing, death and disease — through the frame of the messiest elements of our biology.

Some Thing 2011 is the latest addition to Haig's body-obsessed oeuvre. An abject mass of moving gristle and bone, the robotic sculpture draws on the prosthetic aesthetic of B-grade 'body horror' films of the 1970s and 1980s. Presented on a white table, inspired by a morgue, the work's raw clutch of exposed viscera is an unsettling amalgam of gestation, mutation and consciousness; it is an ambiguous form caught in a tenuous struggle between life and death. The shape twitches, jerks and pulsates, its gentle breathing both compelling and monstrous, drawing us into the corporeal drama. Haig states:

> *Some Thing* represents the unclassifiable body, a body that slips out of the comfortable category of what we think of as human. In an attempt to describe accurately what this pulsating mass of melted flesh and guts actually is, the title *Some Thing* seems like an appropriate starting point. It is a body that was possibly once human and is now on its way to being something else, transformed into another thing. Then again this thing could be sub human or post human. We can't quite be sure.[1]

The concept of the body in a state of transmutation is central to *Some Thing*. Haig cites the works of writer William S Burroughs, in particular his third novel, *Naked Lunch* 1959, and the body horror films of director David Cronenberg as key influences. Described by the artist as 'a creature without a species', *Some Thing* gives form to Burroughs's hallucinatory descriptions of flesh liquefying, transforming and consuming itself in gestation. This 'unidentified tissue', in Burroughs's words, summarises an entity in flux, an aberration of flesh, guts and cartilage, no longer human, while Cronenberg refers to 'the body dissolving boundaries between inside and out, self and other, and the living and the dead'.[2]

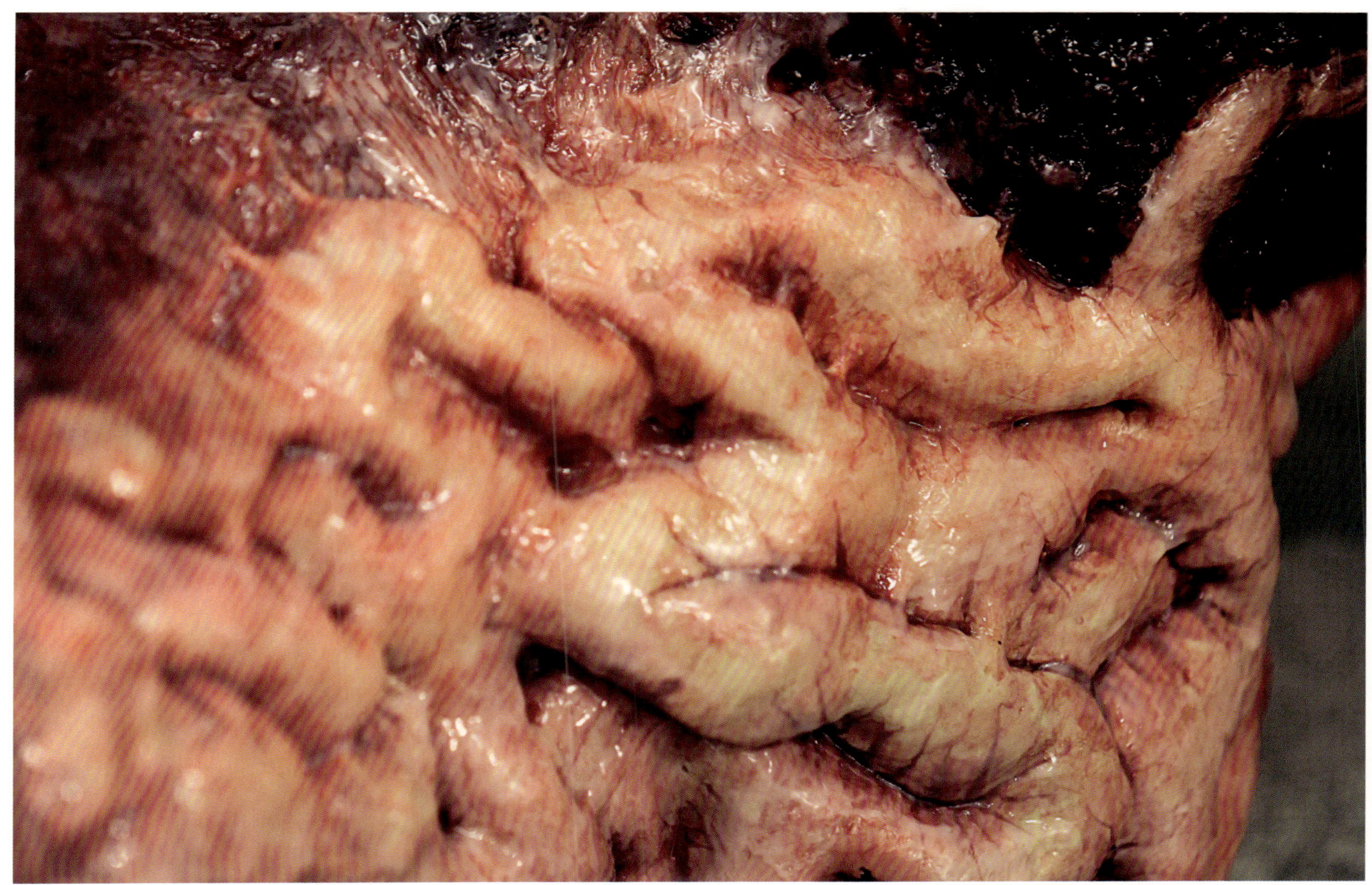

Some Thing (details) 2011

Cronenberg defines these profoundly visceral and grotesque aberrations as 'new flesh'. Recalling a line of dialogue from *Videodrome* 1983 ('Long live the new flesh'), *Some Thing* encapsulates the mutability of flesh as it merges with both physical and biological technologies, demonstrating Cronenberg's fascination with the breakdown and reforming of molecular structures. As illustrated in the ill-fated transportation of matter from one teleportation device to another in Cronenberg's *The Fly* 1986, *Some Thing* literally peels back the layers of skin, muscle and tissue, exposing a mass of vulnerable, twisted remains to the world. As Haig says:

> *Some Thing* not only takes its visceral aesthetic from the horror movie but one also expects to see such a gory prosthetic and pulsating bodily form within the world of a movie and not the real world, i.e., John Carpenter's *The Thing* or Stuart Gordon's *Re-animator*. The illusionary world of film fuses here with the real in the uncanny material of a strange cinematic object. The telepod of cinema delivering the work into the real world, cinema made flesh.[3]

Haig's flagrantly meaty work puts into physical form a key tenet of low-budget, body horror films, namely the depiction of an aberrant growth, accentuating the distinction between the world as we understand it and an abstracted reality. These themes are metaphors for the fundamental human fears of ageing, sickness and mortality. They reflect a fascination with our own flesh and make visible our unconscious horror of the fear that we carry the biological seeds of our own destruction within our own form.

Some Thing is the embodiment of these horrors; it externalises our fears of a body irrevocably changed. Drawn from cinematic roots, *Some Thing*'s simulation of organic reality encourages us to contemplate our bodies and our selves, lending the structure a sympathetic resonance. Caught between gestation and demise, *Some Thing* lies in suspended animation, its place in the life cycle uncertain. From time to time, it twitches to life, pulsing and breathing, waiting for the next step on its evolutionary path. Accompanied by a scratchy, percussive soundtrack by PH2 (Philip Brophy and Philip Samartzis), Ian Haig's *Some Thing* is a powerful and confronting sensory experience.

Amanda Slack-Smith

Endnotes

1 Ian Haig, 'Dr Benway, from Burroughs to Cronenberg: Notes on the work *Some Thing*', *21c Magazine: The Future is Here*, <http://www.21cmagazine.com/Dr-Benway-Notes-on-Some-Thing>, viewed 1 May 2012.

2 Chris Rodley (ed.), *Cronenberg on Cronenberg*, Faber and Faber, London, 1997, p.80.

3 Haig.

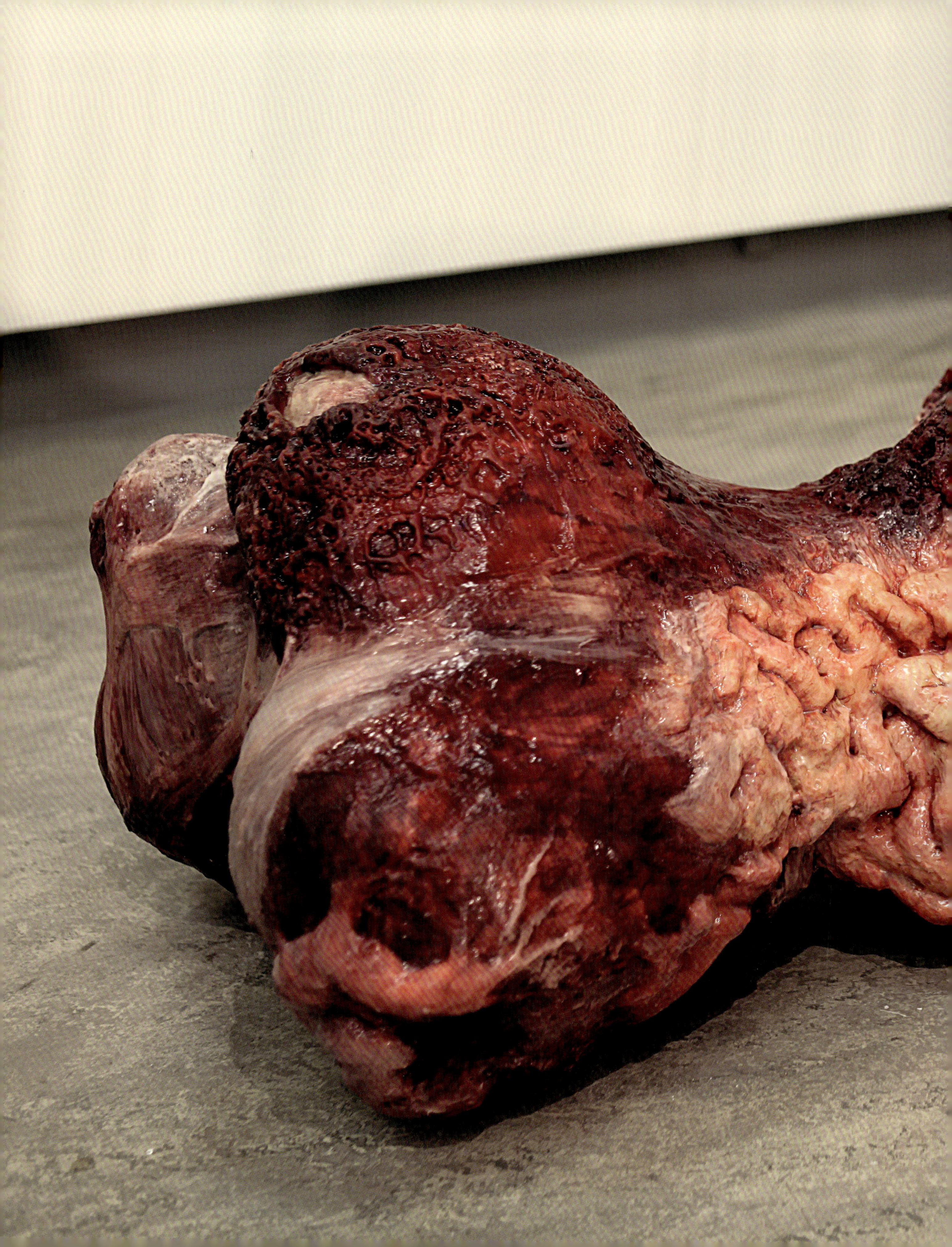

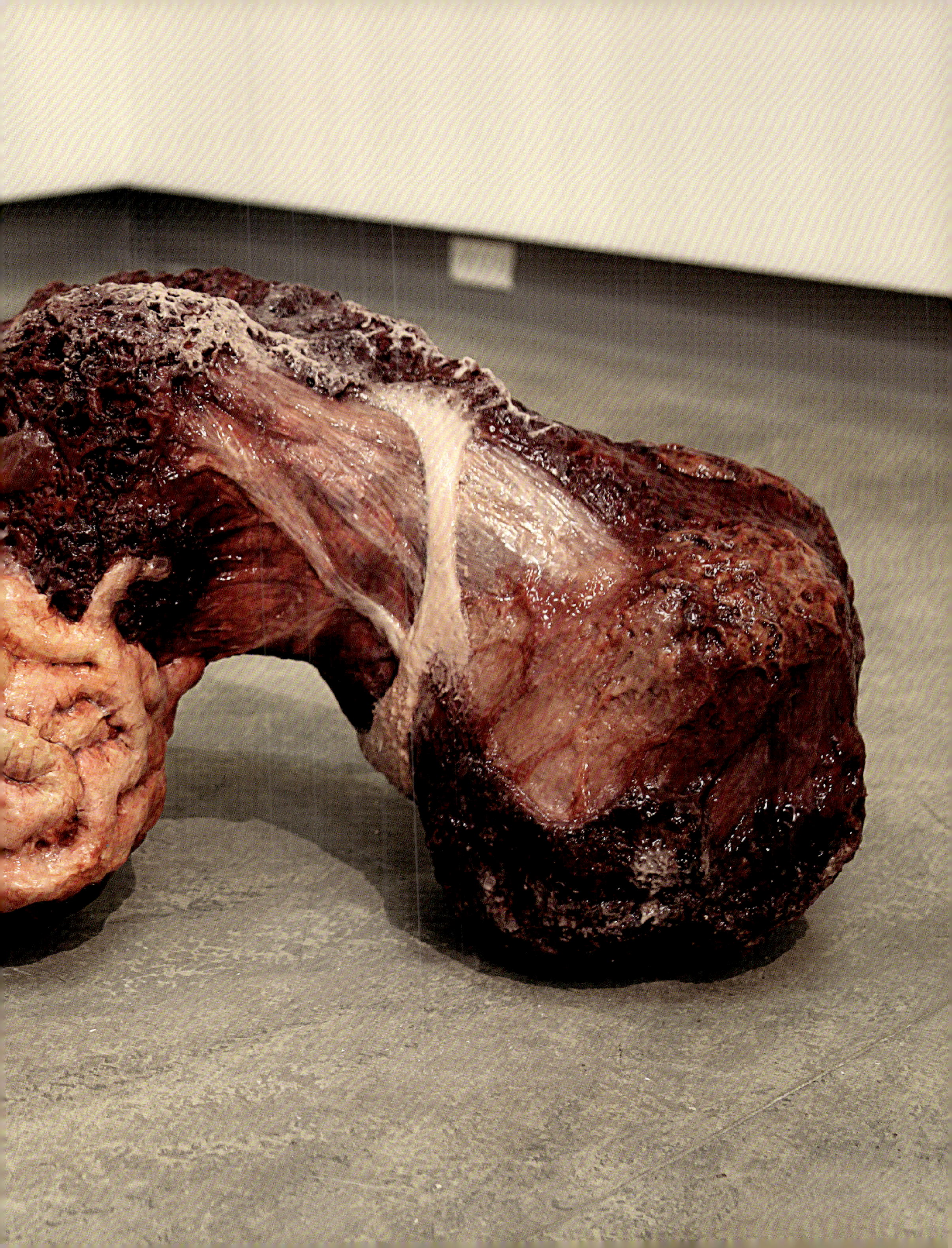

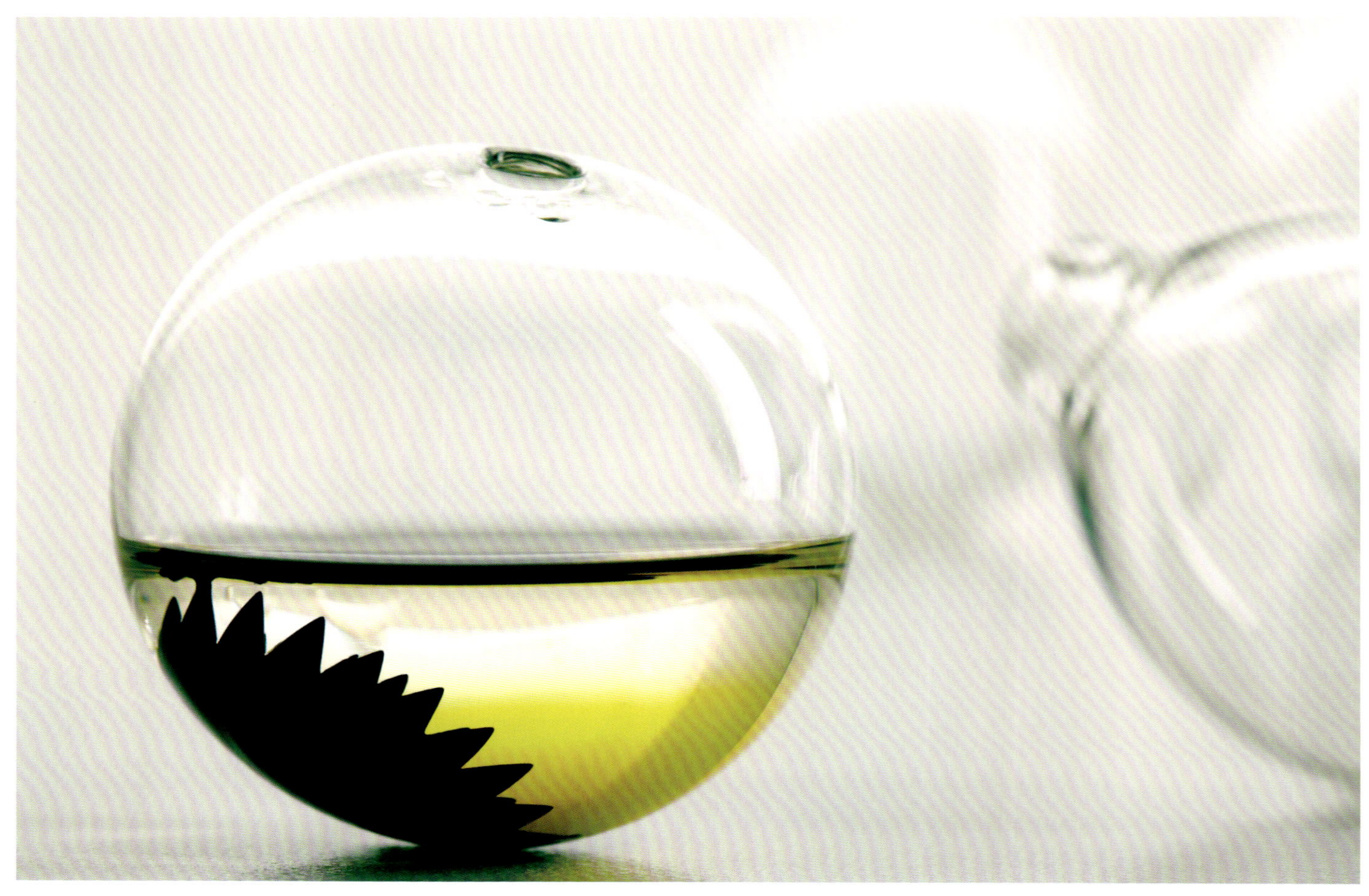

Leah Heiss

Between art and science

Leah Heiss is one of an increasing number of artists working collaboratively with scientists developing advanced technologies. Her interdisciplinary practice is concerned with humanising technology and harnessing the creative possibilities of next generation materials to encourage dialogue and understanding. In this pursuit, Heiss has worked at the research and development stages to develop therapeutic design prototypes, and she explores the potential of these new materials within her art practice.

In a now infamous Rede Lecture at the University of Cambridge in 1959, scientist and novelist CP Snow described the distance and lack of dialogue between the 'two cultures' of science and literature in the following terms:

> Literary intellectuals at one pole — at the other scientists, and as the most representative, the physical scientists. Between the two a gulf of mutual incomprehension — sometimes (particularly among the young) hostility and dislike, but most of all lack of understanding.[1]

More than half a century later, we understand that while science and the arts are intrinsically different, they share many of the same concerns.[2] The proliferation of art–science exhibitions and science-based artist residencies, such as Collide@CERN, offers technology, research and funding possibilities from science, and reflects the growing recognition that both fields have much to offer the other.

In 2007, Heiss undertook a residency with Nanotechnology Victoria, a research and development foundation for the commercialisation of those technologies generated from nanoscience. This invisible technology is already present in our everyday lives — re-mineralising toothpaste, sunscreen and house paint are some common consumer products that use it. In addition, nanotechnologies have the potential to offer major benefits in the fields of medical science and energy generation. In her work developing design solutions for new therapeutic technologies, Heiss created a wearable device capable of removing arsenic from contaminated water, as well as jewellery housing transdermal insulin patches, replacing syringes for drug delivery in the treatment of diabetes. More than simply creating prototypes, these projects were case studies for medical innovation informed by creative art practice at the outset of scientific development, as Heiss says:

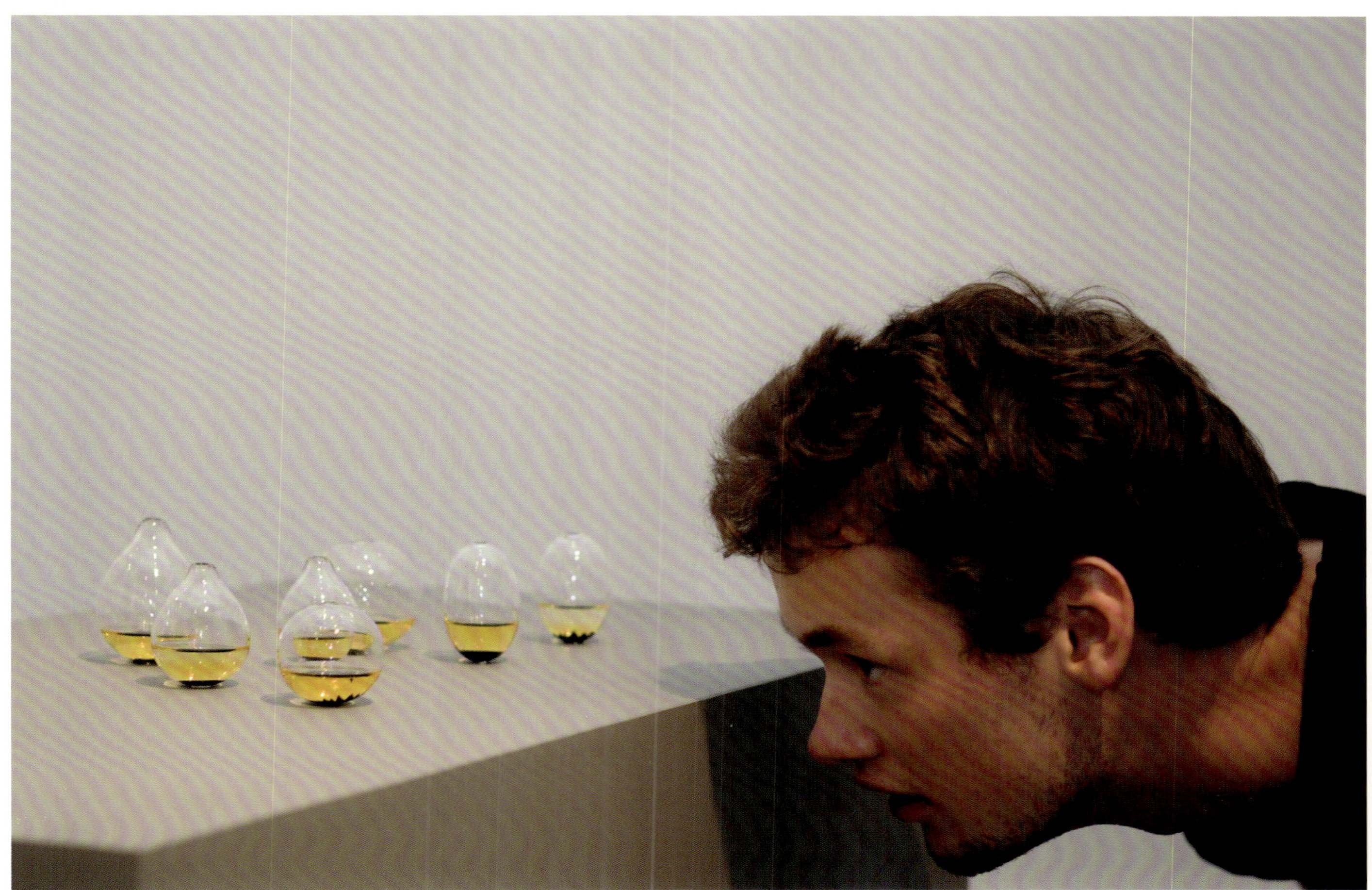

Polarise (details) 2009

Right: installation view, fortyfivedownstairs, Melbourne

Photographs: Narelle Sheean

> Artists tend to think beyond technology to consider whole-of-life human experience — the users, situations, environments etc. — in which the technology will be used . . . Artists ask 'human' questions that allow technologies to become more sensitive to users' needs.[3]

With *Polarity* 2012, an extension of the *Polarise* series begun in 2008, Heiss's experience working with nanomaterials feeds into her practice, fulfilling the cycle of knowledge-sharing and inquiry between art and science. *Polarity* presents nano-scale iron particles captured in a cluster of delicate glass vessels. In its natural state, the magnetic liquid, or ferrofluid, lies inert at the bottom of the vessels, submerged in a protective layer of water and ethanol. However, the creation of a magnetic field causes the liquid to transform into an array of spikes as the material realigns along the magnetic field lines. Captured in Heiss's constellation of tiny glass aquariums, the unrecognisable substance takes on surprising and organic-looking forms; small, spiky creatures randomly appear and dissolve with the magnetic pulse.

This magnetic liquid has a broad range of practical applications and is commonly used in mechanics, electronics and advanced medical techniques. In its quiet and refined movement, *Polarity* distils the material and removes it from its utilitarian functions. Ferrofluid, one of the few visible nanomaterials, is often used to illustrate magnetic fields in nanotechnology; however, the mechanisms producing the magnetic field and activating the liquid in the vessels in *Polarity* are carefully concealed within the table so viewers cannot easily tell what, or who, is causing the material to transform. This, as Heiss explains:

> . . . puts the onus back on the viewer to interpret and try to make sense of the vessels and their behaviours. Largely unknown in the non-scientific world, ferrofluid has unique physical and behavioural characteristics and this further compels the viewer to attempt to understand the experience they are engaged in.[4]

This phenomenon is the most basic outcome of an advanced technology, and *Polarity*, the result of material-led investigations, demonstrates the artist's desire to share her curiosity with audiences. With advances in science being made at unprecedented speeds, Leah Heiss's *Polarity* sits outside, or perhaps amid, societal concern regarding new technologies such as engineered nanomaterials. Science is not the subject of inquiry here: Heiss deals with nanomaterials on a human scale, working with the invisible forces of quantum mechanics to create something playful, subtle and mysterious.

Zoe De Luca

Endnotes

1 CP Snow, 'The two cultures', *Leonardo*, vol.23, no.2–3, 1990, pp.169–73.

2 Snow's original thesis, as well as his revised proposal of a 'third culture' to foster dialogue between the two factions, now considered to be science and the arts more broadly, is discussed at length in the recent publication: Carafoli Ernesto, Gian Antonio Danieli and Giuseppe O Longo (eds.), *The Two Cultures*, Springer, Dordrecht, Netherlands, 2009.

3 Leah Heiss, email correspondence with the author, 17 May 2012.

4 Leah Heiss, 'Therapeutic art practice: How experimental art practice can radically inform the development of our therapeutic technologies' [paper 5], *Studies in Material Thinking*, vol.8, May 2012, pp.1–9.

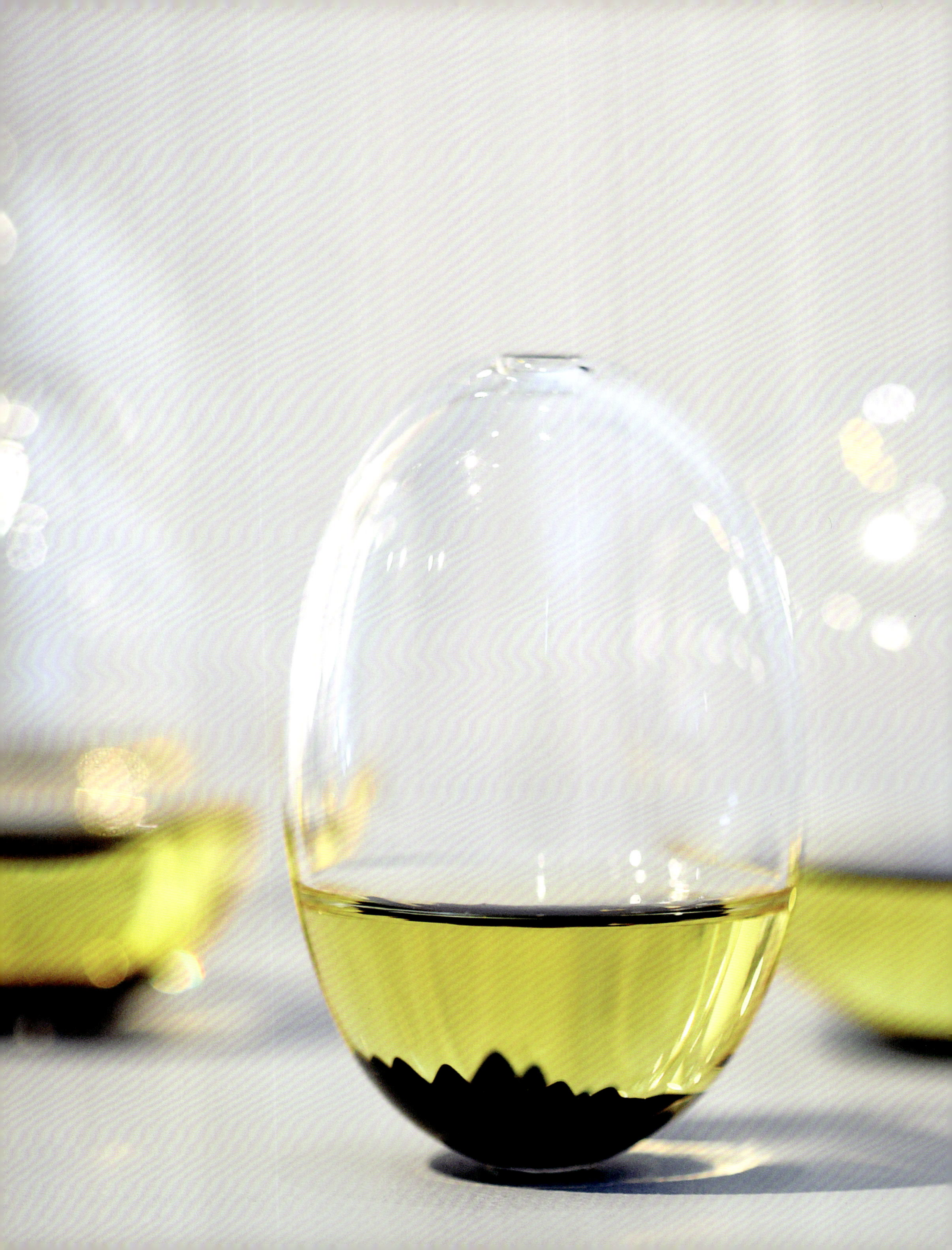

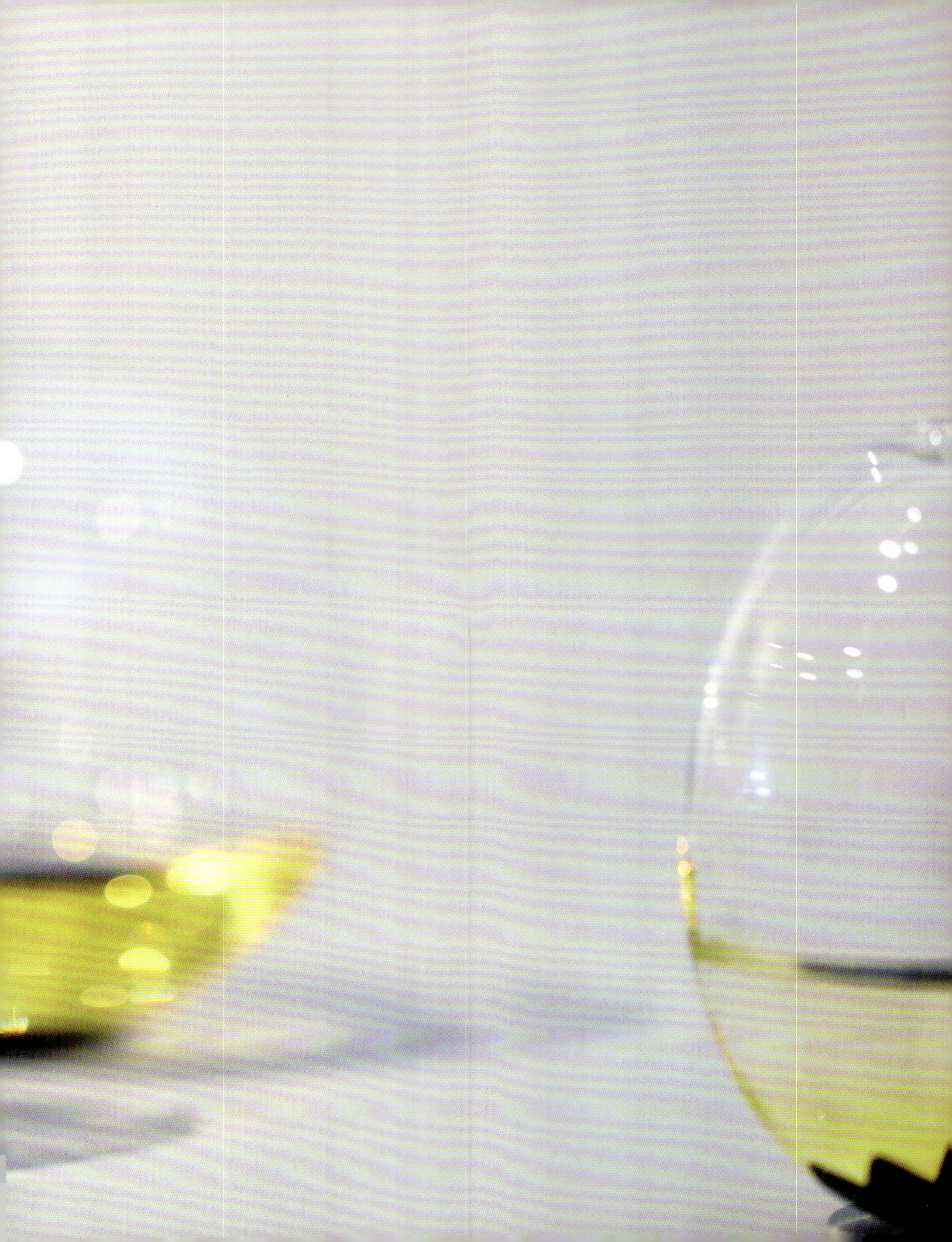

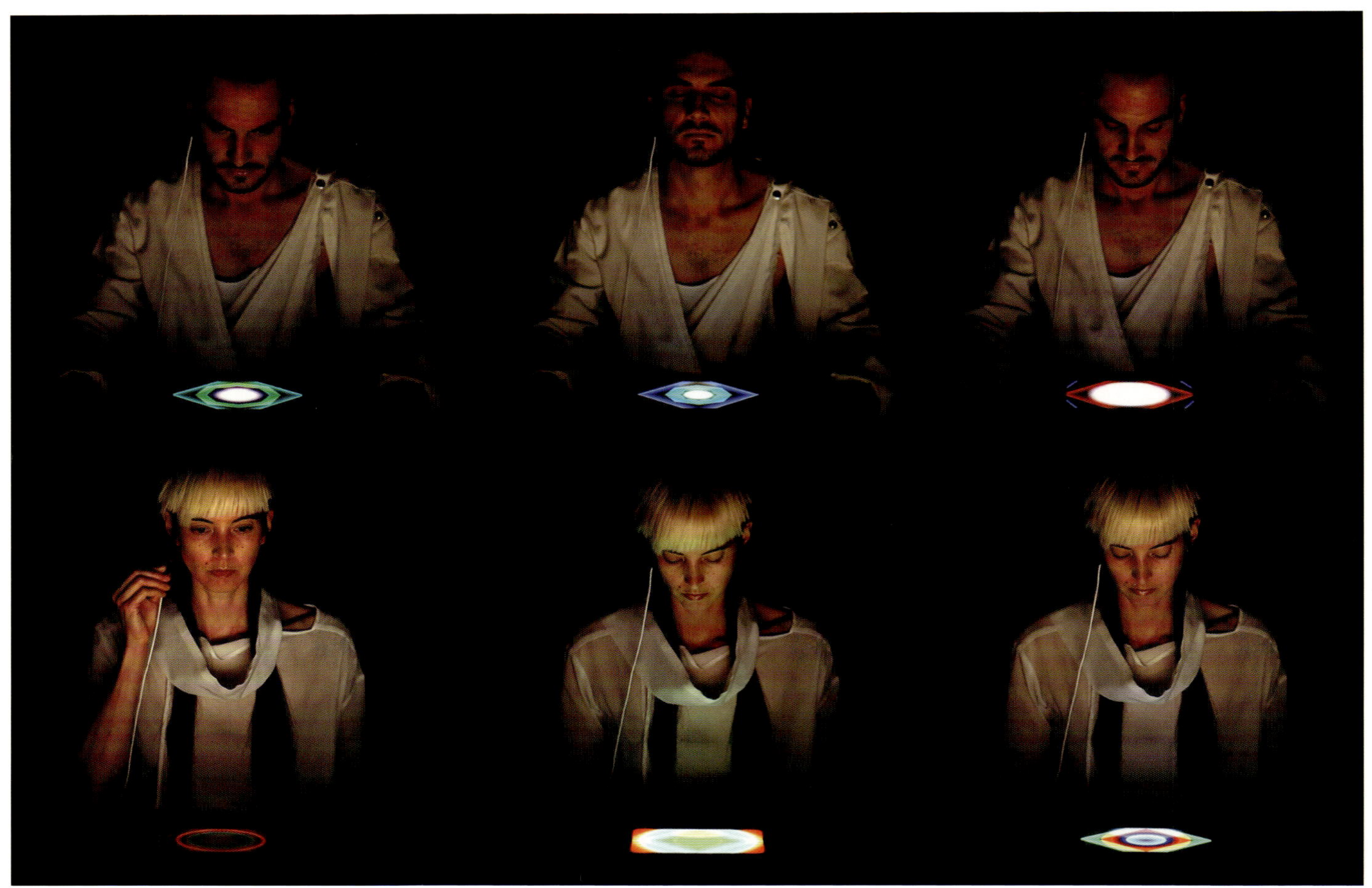

George Poonkhin Khut

Enhanced awareness

The sound of a heartbeat can draw us into the present with a rare strength and swiftness. In placing an ear on another's chest, we get an immediate and arresting sense of the rudimentary elements of being. The intimacy of the moment is heightened with every pulse, and this rhythmic marker of time is a sobering evocation of mortality. Such a powerful experience pierces the stream of distractions vying for our attention and relocates us in the material life. George Poonkhin Khut's practice is attuned to this understanding; to this end, he often involves the audience in his work in order to encourage an awareness of the world that exists uniquely within us all.

Distillery: Waveforming 2012 is the evolution of a project initially developed as an experimental relaxation training system for managing the pain and anxiety experienced by children undergoing recurrent clinical procedures. The hardware is comprised of a clip-on heart monitor and an iPad displaying layers of geometric graphics with an accompanying soundscape.[1] The system's configuration enables the 'sitter' to interact with a live, abstract visualisation of the rhythm of their own heartbeat. Layers of luminous, continually morphing geometric forms create a circular loop of information between body, mind and machine, which is known as biofeedback.

Khut's work, in essence an iPad application or 'app' prototype, invites the audience to explore connections between mental, emotional and physiological phenomena. By combining measured breathing and a quiet mind, users can produce resonant, wave-like oscillations in their heart rate pattern that coincide with a breathing rate of around ten seconds per breath cycle, or six breaths per minute. These pronounced, wave-like changes in heart rate occur spontaneously in many forms of meditation and devotional practice. Thus, otherwise hidden body–mind interactions are now exposed through technology.

Initially developed for use in a medical context at the Kids' Rehab Unit at the Children's Hospital at Westmead, the therapeutic and pedagogical intent of Khut's work is clear. Transferred to a gallery space, the engaging nature of the work presents the opportunity for a uniquely aesthetic experience of one's own life force, and immediate interactions between emotion and physiology.

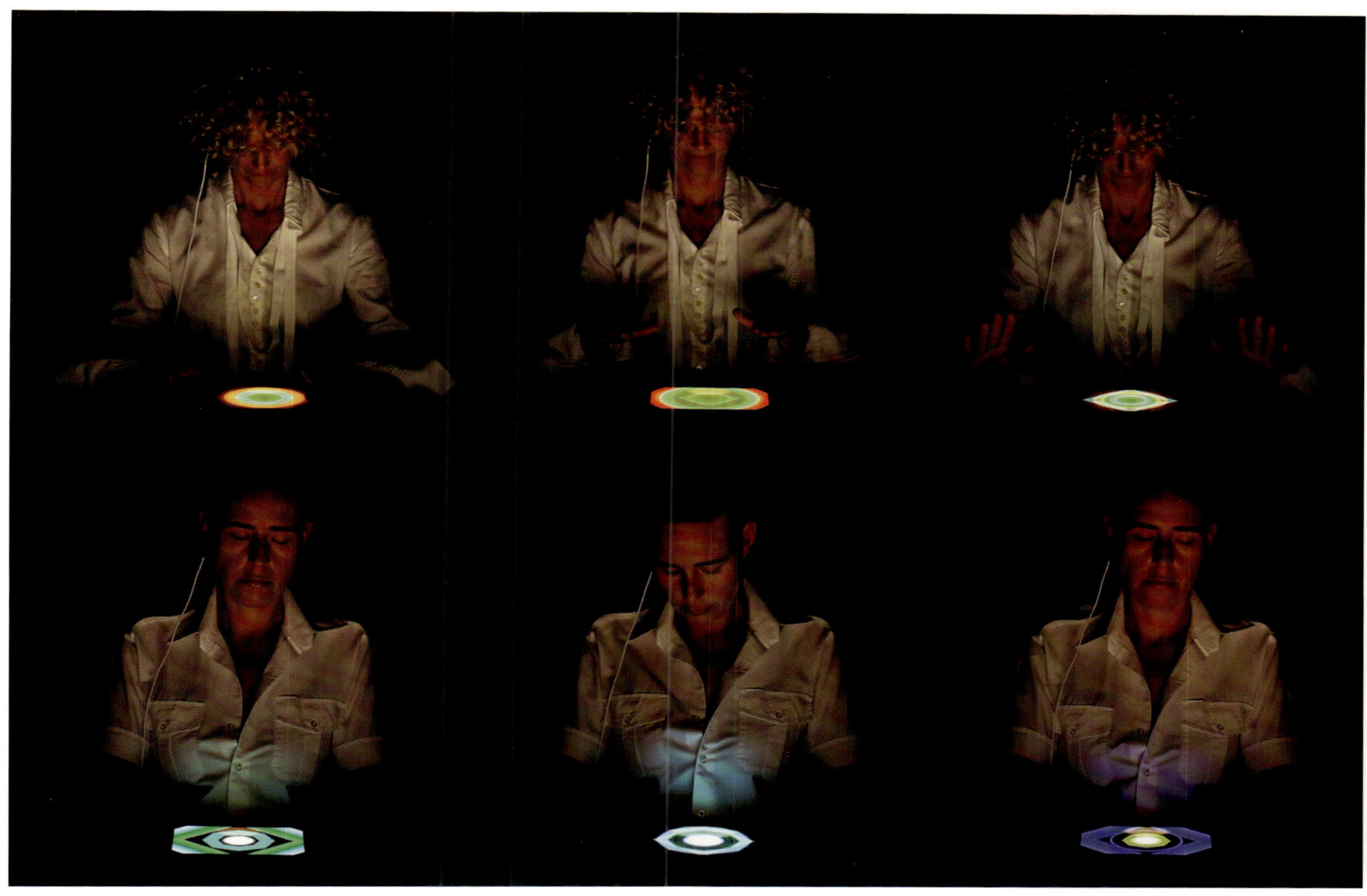

Left: *Distillery: Waveforming (Portrait of Rob, January 2012)* and *(Portrait of Lian, January 2012)* (stills) 2012

Right: *Distillery: Waveforming (Portrait of Barbie, January 2012)* and *(Portrait of Bec, January 2012)* (stills) 2012

Camera: Julia Pendrill Charles; stylist: Troy Brennan

Khut's desire is to focus our attention inwards — to a poetics of attention — and to be aware of our experience of ourselves. This relates to the writings of contemporary philosopher Richard Shusterman and his concept of 'somaesthetics'. This was conceived as a sub-discipline of aesthetics, in which Shusterman attempted to broaden aesthetic experience from its definition as a sensory experience of the outside world to include the 'beautiful experience of one's own body from within — the endorphin-enhanced glow of high-level breathing, the tingling thrill of feeling into new parts of one's spine'.[2] Shusterman believes that the philosophical project of aesthetics — in essence, the distillation of art and the experience of beauty into theoretical terms — has privileged intellectual values and neglected, or actively belittled, the worth of somatic or bodily knowledge. Citing principles held by Socrates, Shusterman argues that Western philosophy has a strong basis in the pursuit of a sound mind and body, and that neglect of our bodies will often translate into deficiencies of both mental and physical health.[3]

Khut's understanding of the historical circumstances we find ourselves in, as articulated by Shusterman, gives rise to his innovative challenge to what he sees as this narrowing of 'art'. While some would argue that expectations of what a body should be are often used as a means of repressing, controlling and exploiting us through oppressive normative models, Shusterman retorts:

> Potent as such indictments may be, they all depend on construing somaesthetics as a theory that reduces the body to an external object — a mechanical instrument of atomized parts, measurable surfaces and standardized norms of beauty. They ignore the body's subject-role as the living locus of beautiful, personal experience. But somaesthetics, in its *experiential* dimension, clearly refuses to exteriorize the body as an alienated thing distinct from the active spirit of human experience. Nor does it necessarily impose a fixed set of standardized norms of external measurement (e.g., optimal pulse) to assess good somaesthetic experience.[4]

Commentary accompanying the suite of video portraits conveys the sitters' thoughts and emotions that emerged during the course of their interaction with the device. Together, George Poonkhin Khut's application and portraits reveal the diversity of our speculations inspired by the enigmatic interactions of mind and body, and the beauty of becoming attuned to these connections. Recognising the subjective encounters of others, we can better comprehend the greater experience we all share.

Peter McKay

Endnotes

1 The iPad app is currently driven by an additional computer that analyses and translates the user's heart rate pattern, but future upgrades will see this operation run within the iPad.

2 Richard Shusterman, 'Somaesthetics: A disciplinary proposal', *Journal of Aesthetics and Art Criticism*, vol.57, no.3, summer 1999, pp.299–313.

3 Shusterman, p.302.

4 Shusterman, p.306.

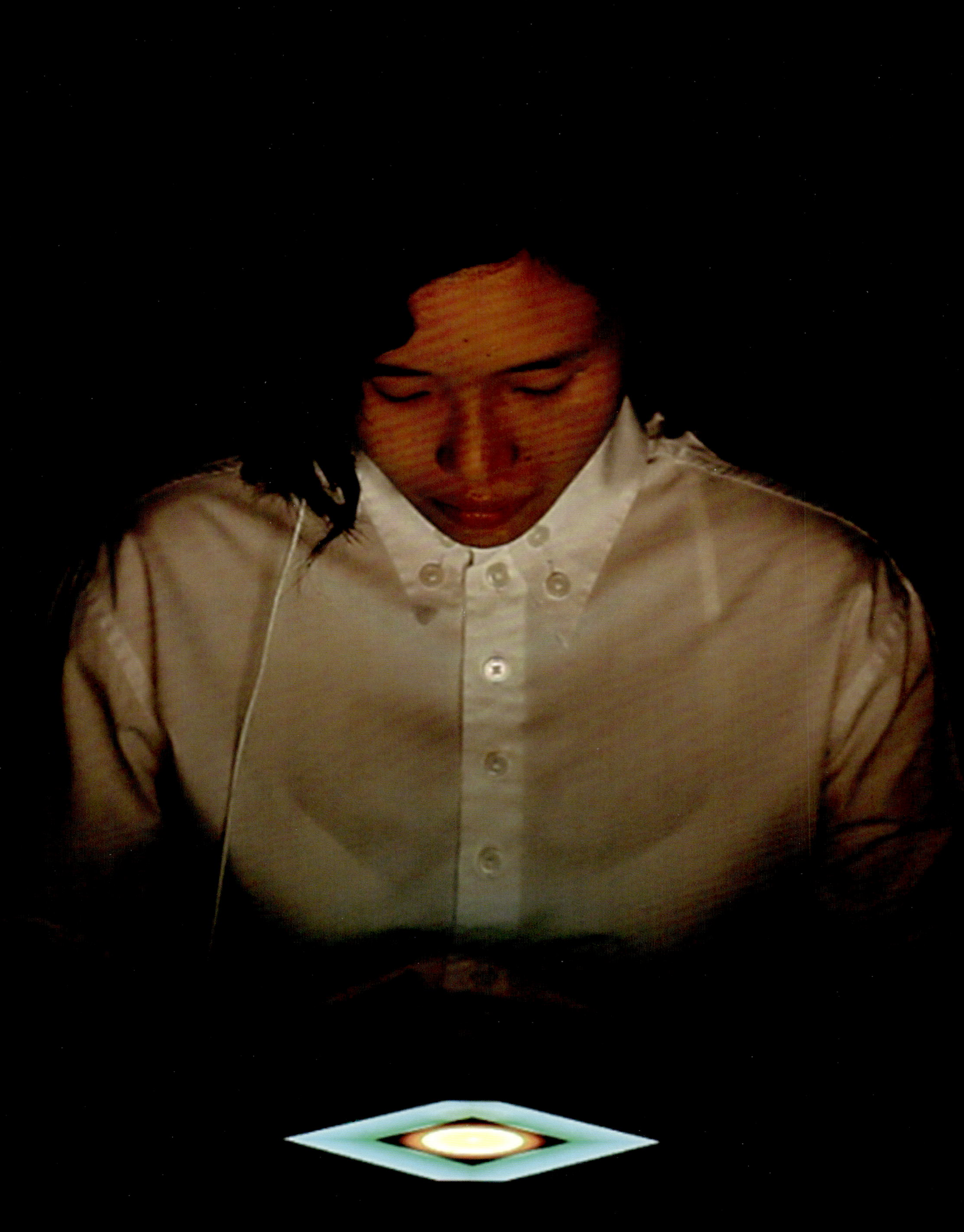

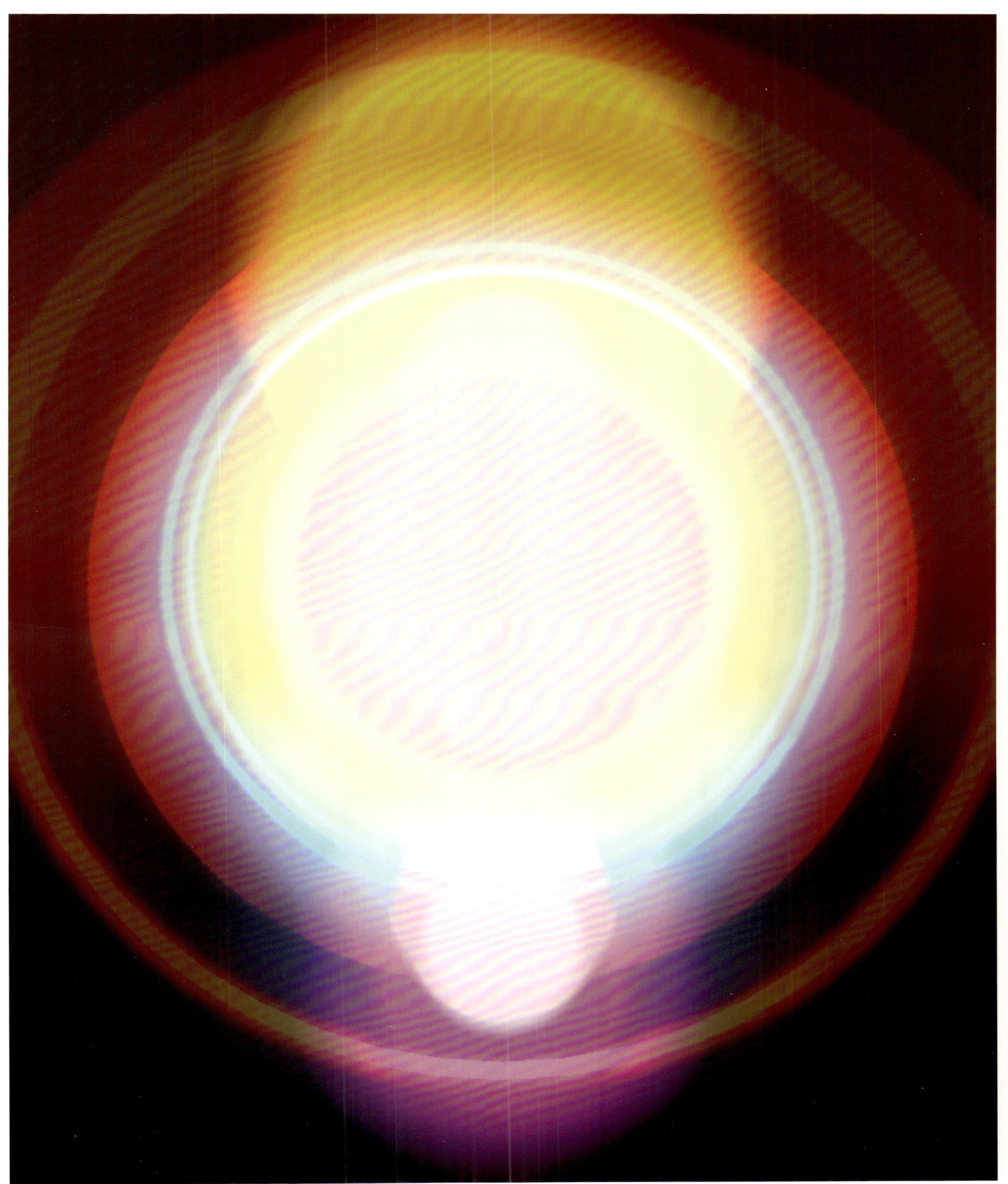

Above: *Distillery: Waveforming* 2012
Screen capture of heart rate controlled iPad app

Opposite: *Distillery: Waveforming (Portrait of Estee, January 2012)* (still) 2012

Camera: Julia Pendrill Charles; stylist: Troy Brennan

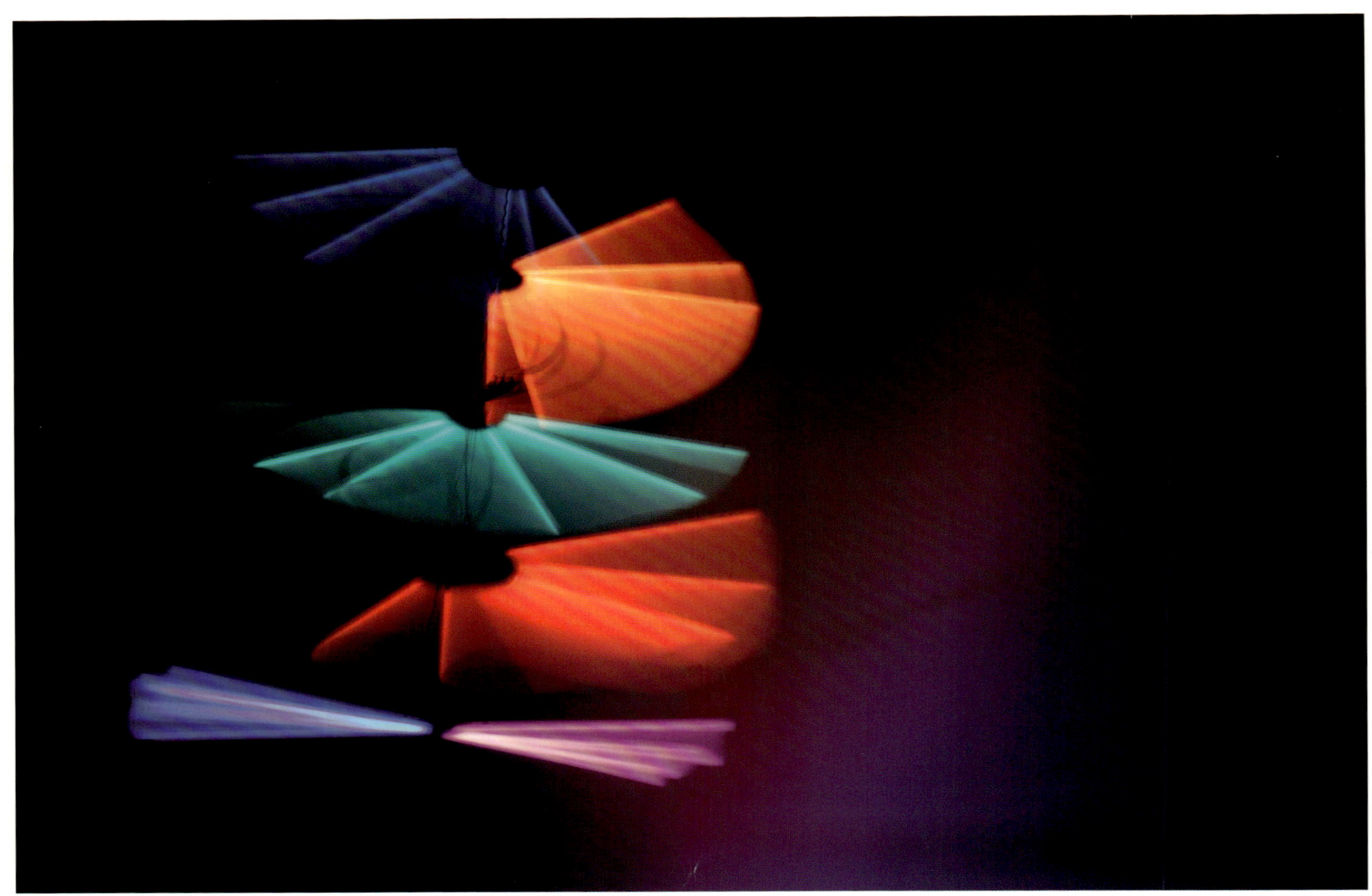

Ross Manning

The waltz of old and new

Ross Manning started creating kinetic sculptures specifically for their sound components, into which environmental influences were often incorporated. It was from his research into soundwaves that he first became interested in light waves, an exploration helped by the practical experiences of his job as a television repairer. Working behind television screens, Manning acquired an understanding of additive colour mixing, a concept central to contemporary screen- and projection-based technologies. In additive colour mixing, different coloured light beams or spectra overlap to produce new colours. For example, white is produced onscreen by equal parts of red, green and blue.

Spectra III 2012, part of an ongoing series, is a mobile sculpture positioned in the centre of a white room, reaching almost from floor to ceiling. Each arm comprises a coloured fluorescent light and a power board, plus an oscillating fan. Each arm is attached off-centre to the one above it — without a central thread, the arms rotate from slightly different axes, spinning with and against the arms above and below. The sculpture recalls television resolution scan lines that have jumped off a screen and are twirling in space.[1] The colours of the fluorescent tubes relate to the colours on the additive colour mixing chart — the lightsfall onto the walls in solid colours and mix as the arms rotate. If, by chance, the lights meet and mix in equal measure, they create white light.

On one wall of the space housing the mobile sculpture, the viewer is presented with three circular apertures. The series of apertures brings to mind the three lenses of a cathode-ray tube (CRT) projector. CRT projectors use additive colour mixing, with red, green and blue lenses each projecting a part of the image, which then combine on screen to produce a full-colour image. Outside the space, the coloured light of the mobile is projected through the apertures and mixes on the white wall opposite. The coloured lights, having passed through the apertures, appear inversely to how they are hung, and their fade rate correlates to their position on the mobile. In this sense, *Spectra III* is a projector reduced to its most basic components.[2]

What is projected onto the wall resembles a natural phenomenon, as if the artist is trying to recreate the aurora australis (the southern lights) within the gallery space. However, the reference point is Sir Isaac Newton's seventeenth-century research into colour refraction,

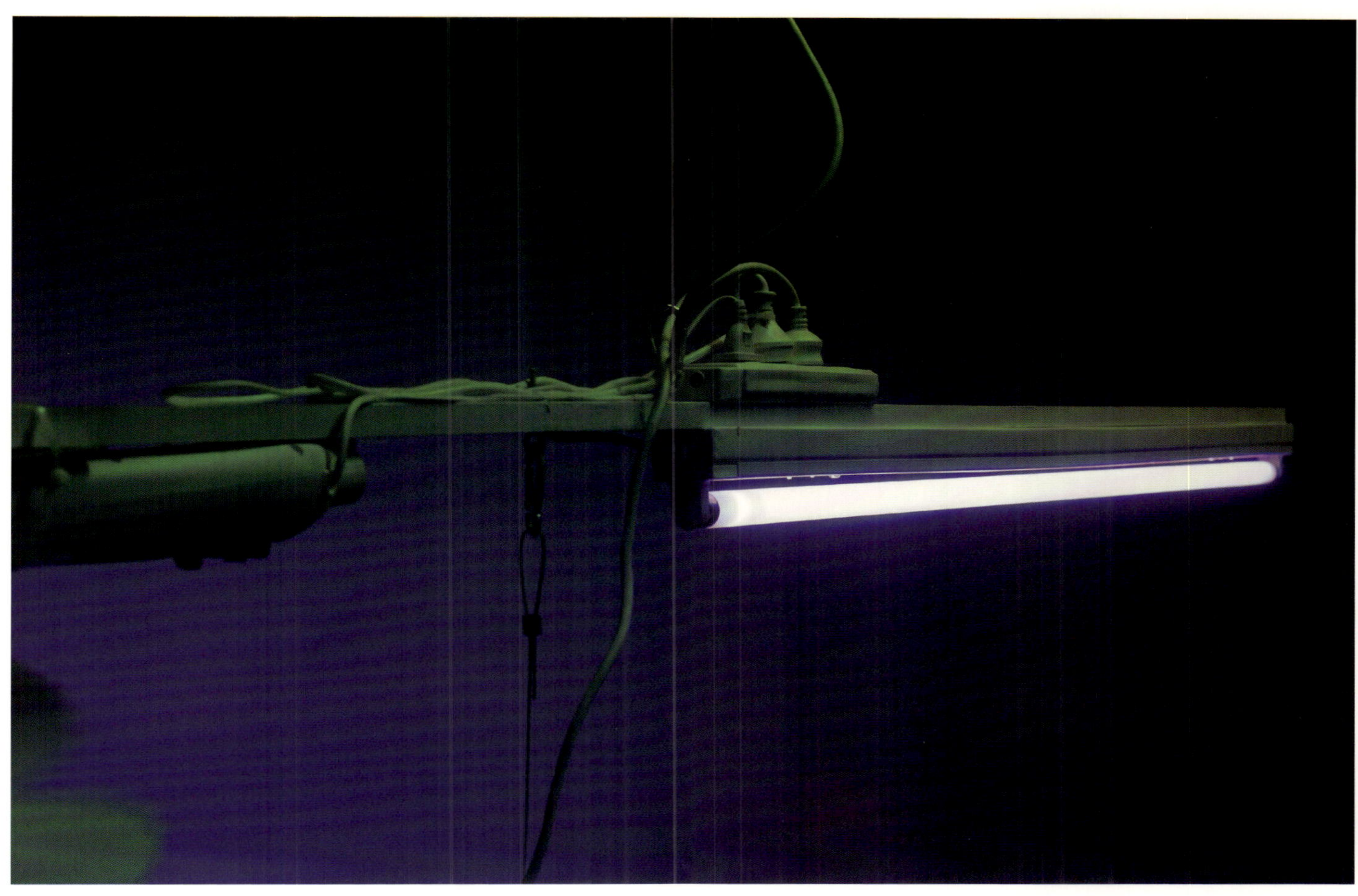

which revealed the way that white light can be refracted into the colours of the rainbow. With *Spectra III*, we see the most basic of optical devices at work (the aperture) alongside the more sophisticated (the CRT projector). To an extent, Manning's works are driven by the input rather than the output of his chosen technology.[3] He approaches all technologies with a similar ease, not seeking a specific piece of equipment because of its ability to produce a particular sound or light composition; instead, he uses the mechanics of a given technology as a point of departure for his explorations.

Manning exposes all the structural components of the work, from the functional power boards to the hooks and wires holding the mobile sculpture together. The fans oscillate in accordance with their speed, but the mobile as a whole doesn't seem to keep a regular rhythm. Without a central axis, the arms softly swing and sway — the mobile appears to move of its own volition.

The rudimentary mechanics of the work do not detract from its power; if anything, they enhance it. Manning plays with the ubiquity of both the fluorescent tube and the household fan, and *Spectra III* sends these common objects whirling and spinning into the realm of magical animism: the work becomes an object with agency that shares our physical space. While Ross Manning's work explores how old and new technologies coexist on a single spectrum, what makes his work so captivating is the life they appear to embody.

Ellie Buttrose

Endnotes

1 Ross Manning, in conversation with the author, 13 April 2012.

2 Manning.

3 Manning.

Left: *Spectra II* (detail) 2012
Installation view; commissioned by the Australian Centre for Contemporary Art for 'NEW12'

Photograph: Andrew Curtis

Right: *Spectra I* (detail) 2012

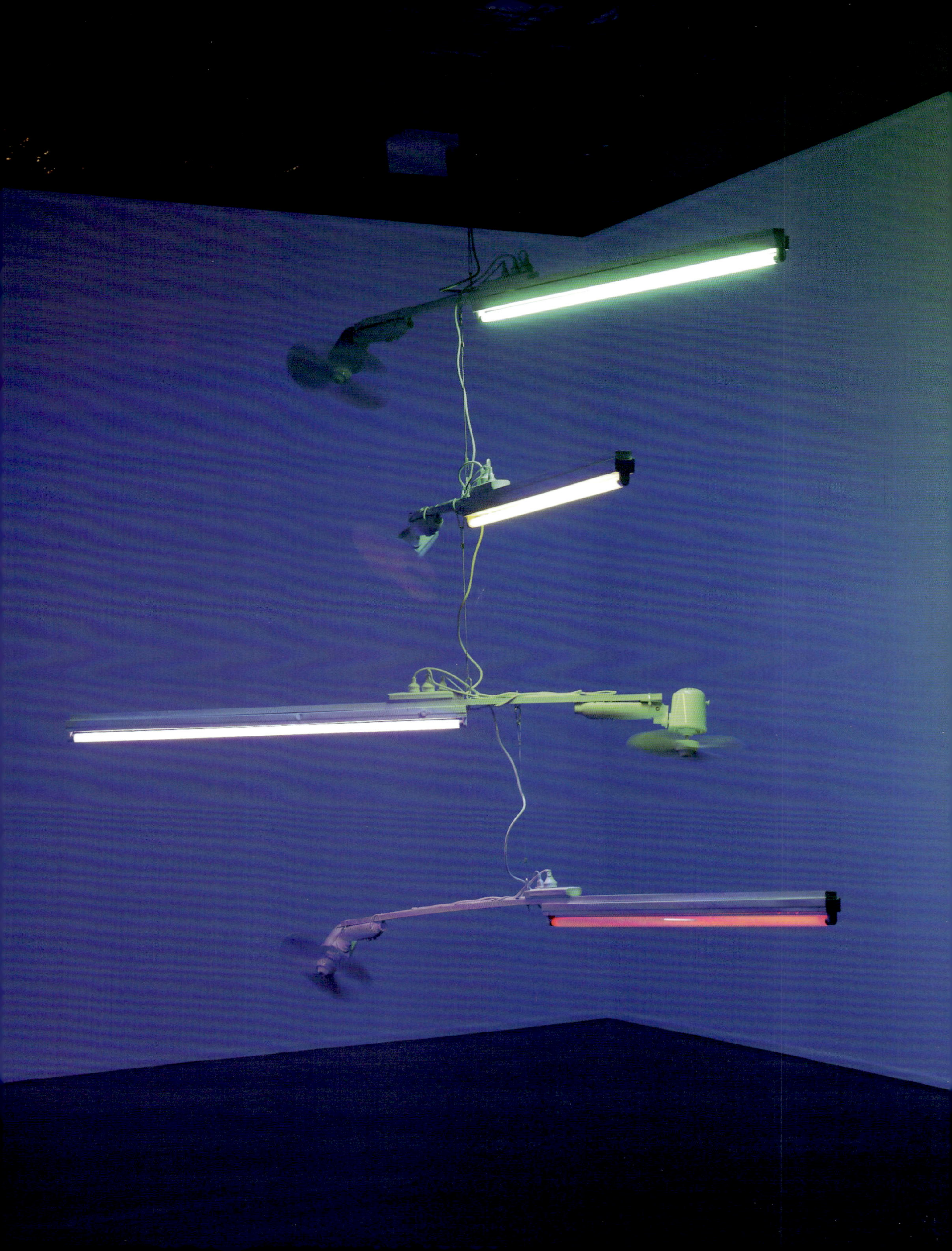

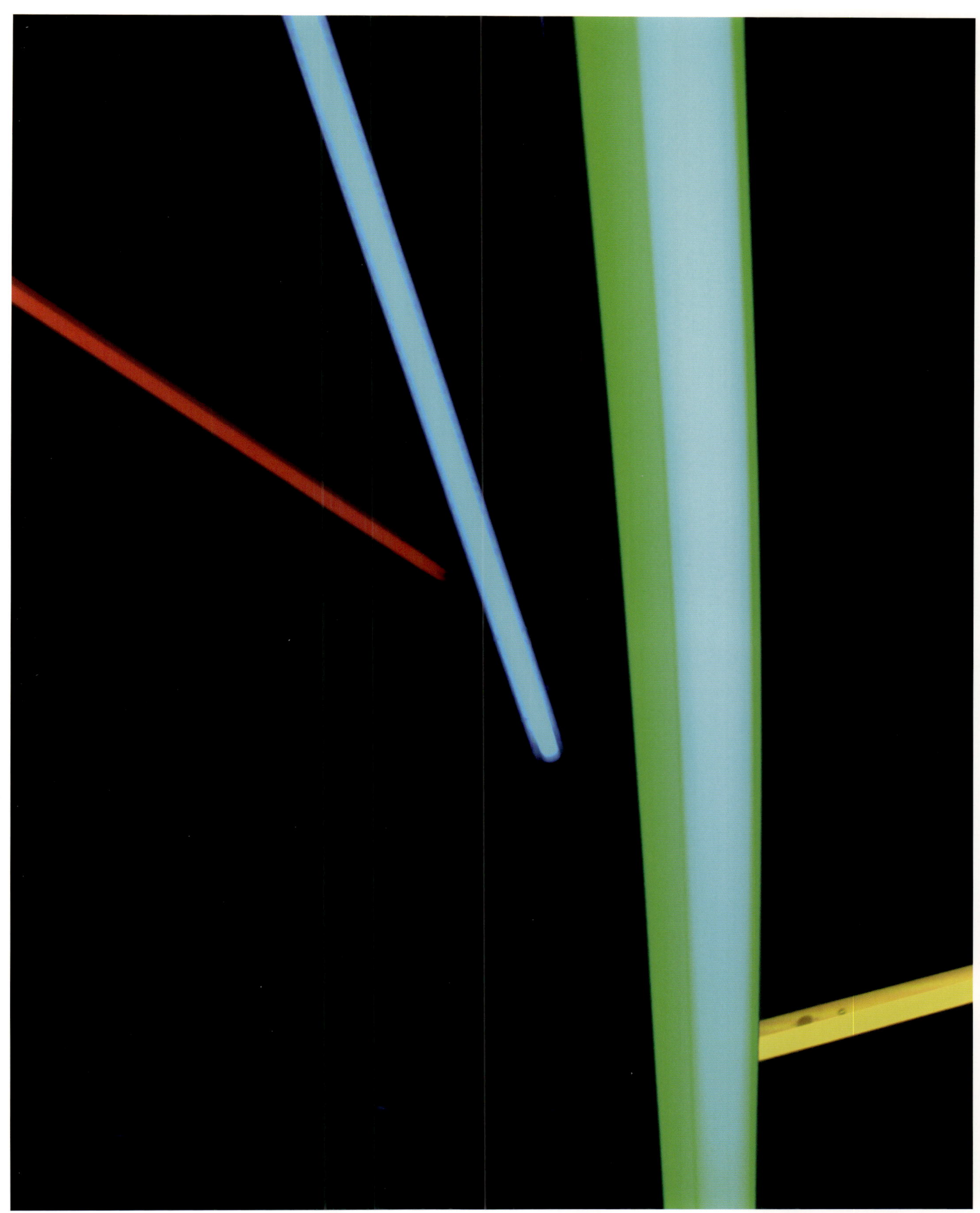

Above: *Spectra I* (detail) 2012

Opposite: *Spectra I* 2012
Installation view, Milani Gallery, Brisbane

ARTIST BIOGRAPHIES

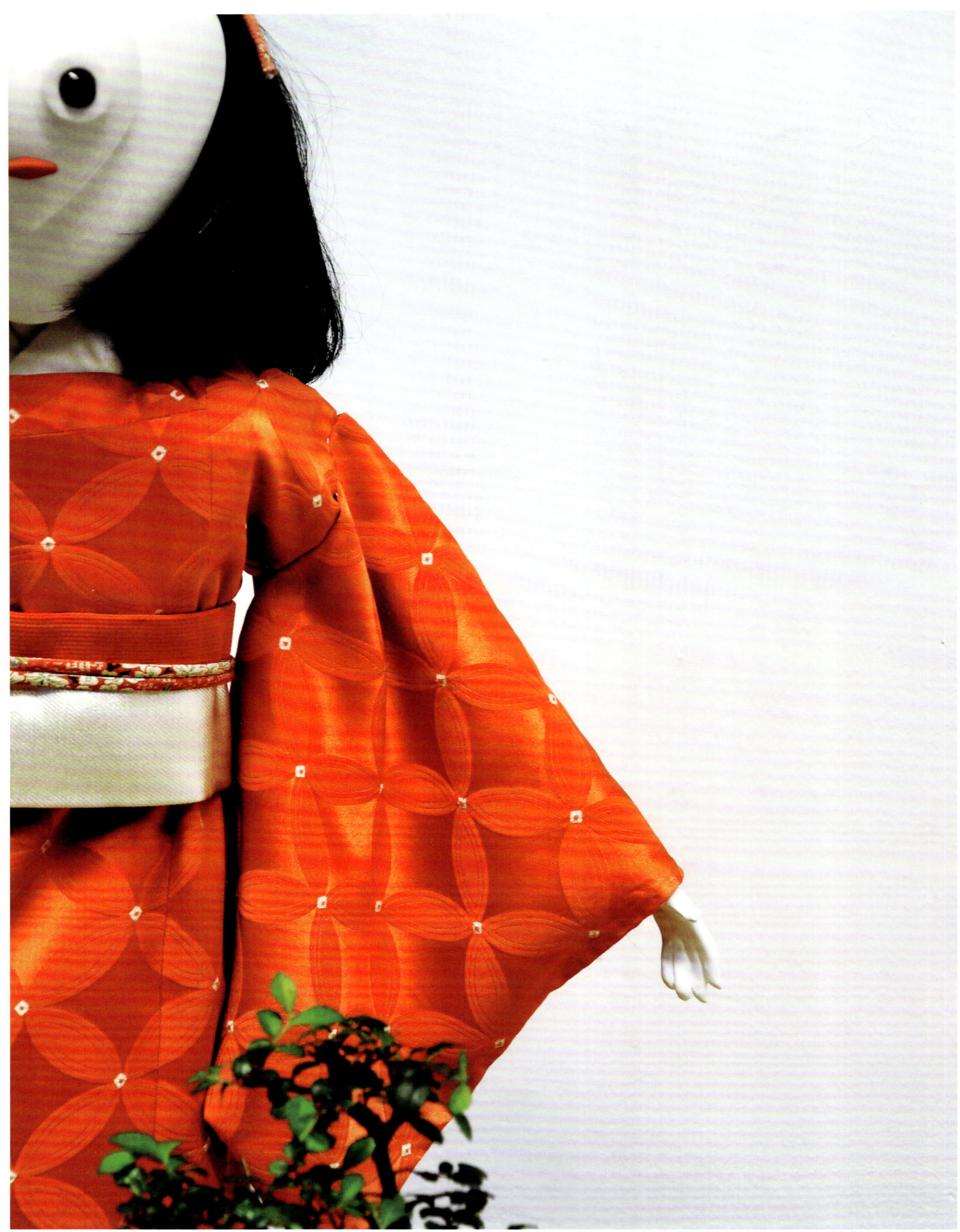

Kirsty Boyle

b.1975 Tamworth
Lives and works in Brisbane and Japan

Tree ceremony (detail) 2010
Programming assistance: Max Lungarella; sound design: Iris Rennert;
assistance: Effie Tanner, Pascal Supratro Schmid
Robotics, microcontroller, infra-red sensors, custom software, wood, textiles, straw, bonsai
90 x 100 x 190cm
Commissioned 2010 by Museum Tinguely, Basel, and Kunsthaus Graz
Courtesy: The artist

SOLO EXHIBITIONS

2009 'Artist in Residence', MedienKunstLabor, Kunsthaus Graz, Austria
2006 'Robot Culture', Consulate-General of Japan, Melbourne
2004 'karakuri', Next Wave Festival, Melbourne
2003 'karakuri.info', WestSpace Gallery, Melbourne

SELECTED GROUP EXHIBITIONS

2011 '111 Selbstversuche', Dock18, Zurich
'Seven with Another', Substation No.4, Brisbane
'Signs of Life: Robot Incubator', 17th International Symposium of Electronic Arts (part of the 12th Istanbul Biennial's Parallel Program exhibition 'Uncontainable'), Cumhuriyet Art Gallery, Maksem, Turkey
'Puppen Projektionsfiguren in der Kunst' ('Figures of Projection in the Arts'), Museum Villa Rot, Burgrieden, Germany
'EcoSapiens', 160 Devonshire St, Taranaki, New Zealand
2010–11 'Robot Dreams', Museum Tinguely, Basel, Switzerland (in parallel with Art Basel) and Kunsthaus Graz, Austria (in conjunction with the 2010 Steirischer Herbst Festival)
2010 'X' (with Natalie Jeremijenko and Remnant/Emergency ArtLab), University of Technology Sydney Gallery, Sydney
'Love the Robots', Dock18, Zurich
2009 'Love the Robots', Dock18, Zurich
'Social Machines', MedienKunstLabor, Kunsthaus Graz, Austria
'Interactivos? '09: Garage Science', Medialab Prado, Madrid
2006 'Traditions and Departures: Highlighting Japanese Influences in Australian Craft and Design', Australia Japan Year of Exchange Exhibition, Craft ACT, Canberra, and Cowra Art Gallery, NSW
2005–06 'Otakulture', Electrofringe Festival, Rocket Art Gallery, Newcastle, NSW; The Whitehouse, Brisbane; Manning Regional Art Gallery, Taree, NSW
2005 'Art and Heart', Curious Eidolon, Melbourne
2004 'Mechalust', Straight Out of Brisbane Festival, Institute of Modern Art and TC Beirne Centre, Brisbane
'Replicate Automate Infiltrate', Electrofringe Festival, Newcastle, NSW
2003 'Run_Way Young and Emerging Artists', Australia Council for the Arts, Sydney

SELECTED RESIDENCIES, GRANTS AND AWARDS

2011–12 Artist in Residence, The Edge | Digital Culture Centre, State Library of Queensland, Brisbane
New Grant, Digital Culture Fund, Australia Council for the Arts
Artist in Residence, Floating Land Festival, Boreen Point, Queensland
Artist in Residence, Museum Villa Rot, Burgrieden, Germany
Artist in Residence, EcoSapiens, Taranaki, New Zealand
2010 *Tree ceremony* [commission] for 'Robot Dreams', Museum Tinguely, Basel, Switzerland, and Kunsthaus Graz, Austria
Artist in Residence (with Natalie Jeremijenko and Remnant/Emergency ArtLab), Artspace, Sydney
Guest Artist, Hackteria Lab + Forum, Dock18, Zurich
2009 Artist in Residence, MKL – MedienKunstLabor, Kunsthaus Graz, Austria (with the support of the EACEA (Education Audiovisual and Culture Executive Agency), Projet Culture 2007–2013 of the European Commission)
Residency Support, Inter-Arts Board, Australia Council for the Arts
'Hybrid Art' category (nomination), Prix Ars Electronica, Linz, Austria
2008–09 Artist in Residence and Researcher, AI Lab, University of Zurich
2007 Skills Development Residency, AI Lab, University of Zurich
Synapse Art/Science International Residency Support, Australian Network for Art and Technology and the Inter-Arts Board, Australia Council for the Arts
2006 Skills Development Support, Inter-Arts Board, Australia Council for the Arts
2002 Run_Way Young and Emerging Artists Initiative, New Media Arts Board, Australia Council for the Arts
Karakuri (mechanical doll craft) instruction with Mr Tamaya Shobei IX, ninth-generation *karakuri* master, and mentorship with Professor Yoshikazu Suematsu, Director, Toyota National College of Technology, Japan
1999 Artist in Resident and Researcher, Interactive Information Institute, RMIT, Melbourne

SELECTED BIBLIOGRAPHY

Davis, Anna. 'RUN_WAY', in *Realtime*, no.57, October–November, 2003, p.24.
De Bourbon-Parme, Aude. 'Reves de Robot: L'Art de la Mecanique', in *Art Actuel – Le Magazine de l'Art Contemporain*, September 2010, pp.68–9.
Higson, Rosalie. 'Going where no man has gone before', *Australian*, September 2007.
Jegge, Alexander. 'Traum der Roboter, hat der Mensch Angst' ('Dream of the robot, the human fear'), *Basellandschaftliche Zeitung*, 9 June 2010.
Jones, David. *Mighty Robots: Mechanical Marvels that Fascinate and Frighten*. Annick Press, Toronto and Vancouver, Canada, 2005.
Marzahn, Alexander. 'Museum Tinguely vom geistesleben der maschine' ('Museum Tinguely from the intellectual life of the machine'), *Basler Zeitung*, 9 June 2010.
Mayer, Helmut. 'Androiden wie wir – Das Museum Tinguely in Basel traumt von Robotern' ('Androids like us – The Museum Tinguely in Basel dreams of robots'), *Frankfurter Allgemeine Zeitung*, 17 July 2010.
Mitchell, Natasha, 'Collaborative practice: Part two', *Filter Magazine*, no.68: ART+SCI=4EVA, July, 2008, <http://www.filter.org.au/issue-68/collaborative-practice-an-interview-with-kirsty-boyle/>, viewed 26 June 2012.
O'Reilly, Rachel. 'Mecha-lust, mecha-love', in *Realtime*, no.65, February–March, 2005, p.30.
Rackham, Melinda. 'Divisible Istanbul: ISEA2011', in *Realtime*, no.106, December–January, 2011, p.22.
Richards, Tim. 'I Am Robot', *Age*, 18 April 2005, p.6.

WEBSITES

http://onnai.com
http://karakuri.info

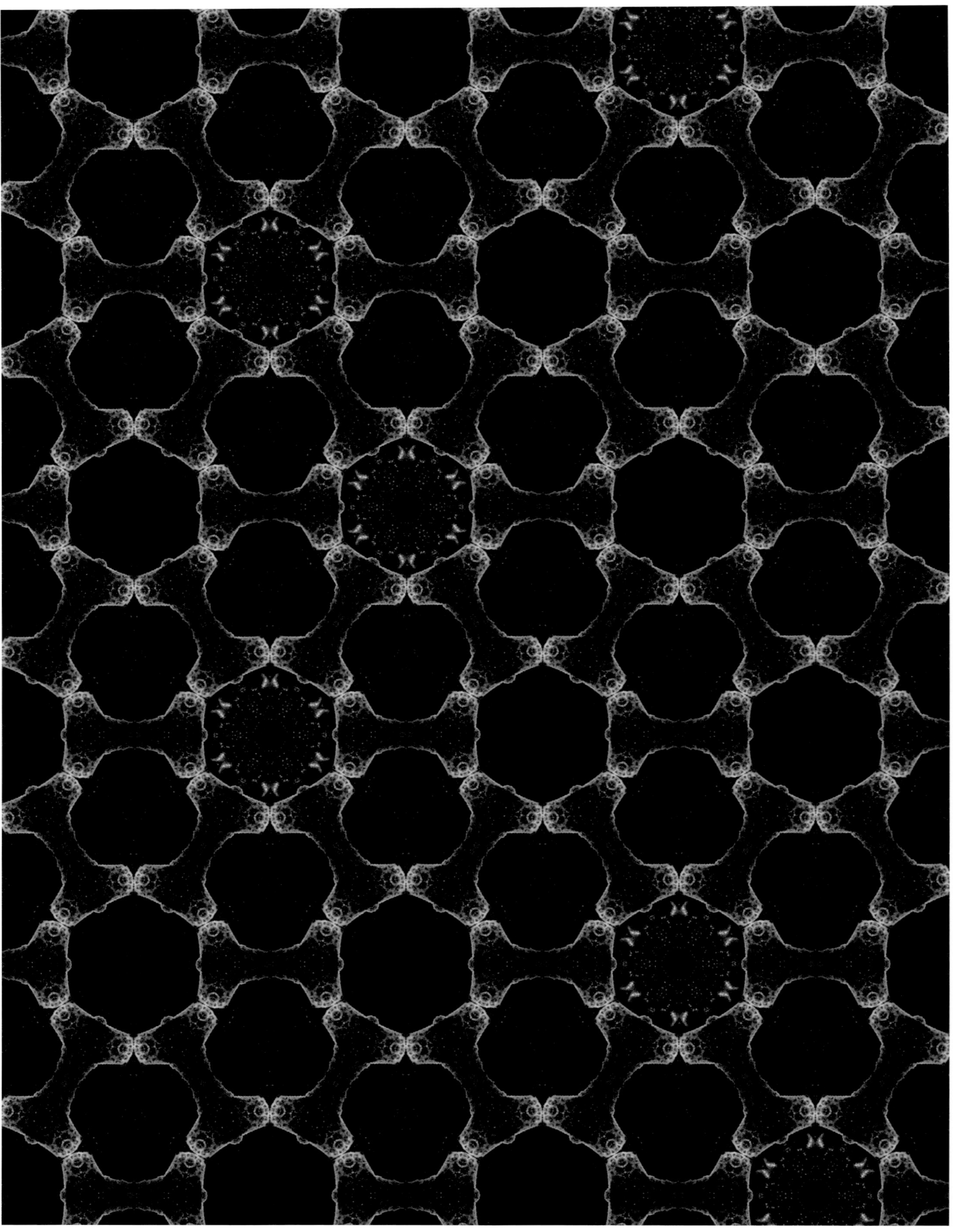

Karen Casey

b.1956 Hobart
Lives and works in Melbourne

Dream zone (digital study, detail) 2012
Technical collaborator and software developer: Harry Sokol;
sound designer: Tim Cole; audiovisual programmer: James Power
Three-channel projection exhibited from computer, audiovisual data rendering in real time, colour, surround sound, ed. 1/3
Courtesy: The artist

SELECTED SOLO EXHIBITIONS

2012	'Reach Out', Lethbridge Gallery, St Martins Central Academy of Fine Arts, London
2011	'Woven Histories: A Gift of Light', Centro de las Artes, San Augustin, Mexico
	'Aotearoa: Hands across the Tasman', Academy of Fine Arts Gallery, Wellington, NZ
	'Karen Casey 02.2011: Global Mind Project', Lea Digital Media Exhibition Platform
2008	'Contact/Converse', Ian Potter Centre, National Gallery of Victoria, Melbourne
	'Mindscapes', Benalla Art Gallery, Victoria
2004–05	'Art of Mind', Darwin Arts Festival, 24HR Art, NT Centre for Contemporary Art, Darwin; RMIT Gallery, Melbourne
2003	'Casting Shadows/Drawing Light', Arc One Gallery, Melbourne
2002	'Ripple', Span Galleries, Melbourne
2000	'Radiant', Span Galleries, Melbourne

SELECTED GROUP EXHIBITIONS

2012	'The World is Everything That is the Case', John Curtin Gallery, Curtin University, Perth
2011	'Uncontainable', International Symposium on Electronic Art 2011, Istanbul
2009	Josephine Ulrick and Win Schubert Photography Award, Gold Coast City Art Gallery, Surfers Paradise, Queensland
2006	'Helen Lempriere Sculpture Award', Werribee Park, Victoria
	'Tribal Expressions', Arts Centre, Melbourne
2004	'Skinned: Yarra Array 2004', City of Melbourne Outdoor Works Biennial
	'Big Spooks', National Gallery of Australia, Canberra
2003	'Via Vai Arte in Valigia', Museo Castello Ducale, Palena, Abruzzo; Basilica di Collemaggio, L'Aquilla, Abruzzo; Palazzo Cisterna, Turin, Italy
2001–02	'Digital Ghosts', Red Gate Gallery, Beijing; Tin Sheds Gallery, University of Sydney
2001	'Art towards Reconciliation', Gernika Peace Museum, Gernika, Spain
1999	'Beyond the Future: The Third Asia Pacific Triennial of Contemporary Art', Queensland Art Gallery, Brisbane

SELECTED PROJECTS, EVENTS AND COMMISSIONS

2011	'Connexion/Confienza' [curator], Centro de las Artes, San Luis Potosi
	TRUST Project, San Augustin, Oaxaca and San Luis Potosi, Mexico
	Let's Shake, Matariki Festival, Te Papa National Museum, Wellington, NZ
2010	'Global Mind Project: Spectacle of the Mind' [artistic director], Federation Square, Melbourne
	'Alternative Worlds' [Australia, Canada, Mexico cultural exchange], RMIT University, Melbourne
	Ripple (commission), TRAC – Thomastown Recreation & Aquatic Centre, Victoria
2008	Australia 2020 Summit: Towards a Creative Future [invited participant], Parliament House, Canberra
2007	*Touchstone for reconciliation* [commission], University of Adelaide
2006–09	Let's Shake [public art events], various venues (ongoing)
2005	Mall redevelopment, City of Moreland [project design team with Hassell Architects]
	Ochre Reef [commission], Collins Towers, Melbourne
2004–05	Art of Mind research project, Brain Sciences Institute, Swinburne University, Melbourne
2003	*Heartland* [commission], Docklands Urban Art, Melbourne

QUALIFICATIONS, RESIDENCIES, GRANTS AND AWARDS

2012	PhD candidate, Monash University, Melbourne
2011	Residency, Centro de las Artes, San Augustin, Oaxaca, Mexico
	Residency, Centro de las Artes, San Luis Potosi, Mexico
2010	Australian Postgraduate Award
2009	Arts Grant, City of Melbourne
2008	AIA Award for Design Excellence [with Hassell Architects]
2007	Development Grant, Arts Victoria
	Wyndham City Council Acquisitive Prize, Helen Lempriere National Sculpture Award
	Multi-artform grant, Inter-Arts Office, Australia Council for the Arts
2004	Development Grant, New Media Arts, Australia Council for the Arts
	Artist in Residence, City of Melbourne

SELECTED BIBLIOGRAPHY

Grishin, Sasha. *Australian Printmaking in the 1990s: Artist Printmakers 1990–1995.* Craftsman House, Sydney, 1996.

Grishin, Sasha. 'Profiles in print: Karen Casey'. *Craft Arts International*, no.63, 2005.

Kleinert, Sylvia and Neale, Margot. *Oxford Companion to Aboriginal Art.* Oxford University Press, Melbourne, 2000.

McCulloch, Susan. *The New McCulloch's Encyclopedia of Australian Art.* Miegunyah Press, Fitzroy, Victoria, 2006.

Mendelssohn, Johanna. '50 of Australia's most collectable artists'. *Australian Art Collector*, no.31, 2005.

Neale, Margo. 'Karen Casey: A moment out of time'. In *Beyond the Future: The Third Asia Pacific Triennial of Contemporary Art* [exhibition catalogue]. Queensland Art Gallery, Brisbane, 1999.

Nicholls, Christine. 'Contested spaces: Handshakes for reconciliation'. *World Sculpture News*, vol.13, no.3, 2007.

Spence, Rachel. 'Seriously contemporary'. *Financial Times*, 23 September 2011, <http://www.ft.com/cms/s/2/1c80635a-e39e-11e0-8990-00144feabdc0.html#axzz1y6r86wbl>, viewed 18 June 2012.

SELECTED COLLECTIONS

Art Gallery of New South Wales, Sydney
Art Gallery of South Australia, Adelaide
Art Gallery of Western Australia, Perth
British Museum, London
Musée du Quai Branly, Paris
National Gallery of Australia, Canberra
National Gallery of Victoria, Melbourne
National Museum of Modern Art, Kyoto
Queensland Art Gallery, Brisbane
Rijksmuseum, Amsterdam

WEBSITE

www.globalmindproject.com

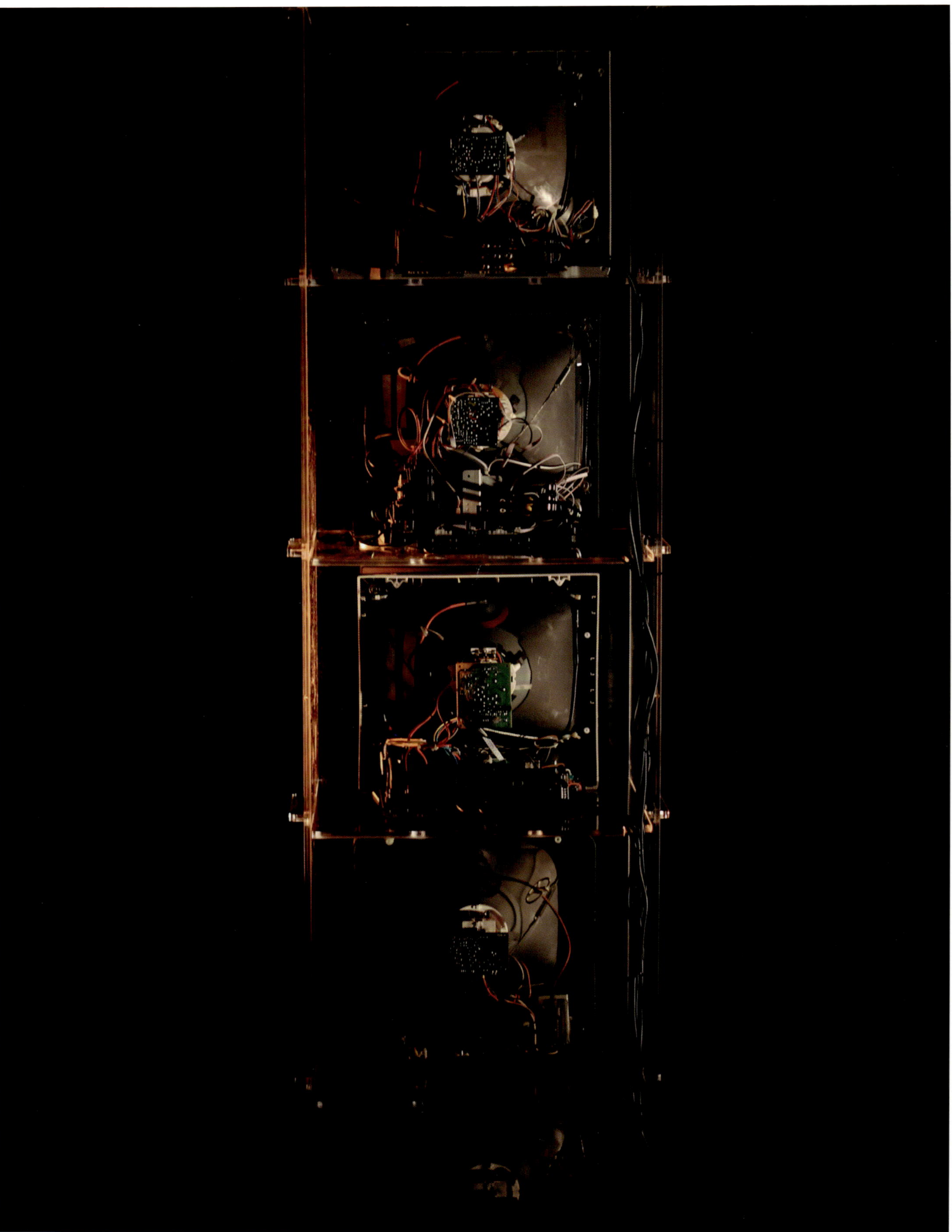

Robin Fox

b.1973 Canberra
Lives and works in Melbourne

CRT: homage to Léon Theremin (detail) 2012
Cathode-ray tube televisions, multichannel sound, motion tracking system, custom software, acrylic glass
Three parts: 207 x 51cm x 62cm (each)
Courtesy: The artist

SELECTED EXHIBITIONS AND INSTALLATIONS

2012 'zero-crossing laser and multi-channel sound', Long Gallery, Salamanca Arts Centre, Hobart
'Giant Theremin', Les Erdi Plaza, Melbourne
2011 'Volta', Gesellschaft für Kunst und Gestaltung, Bonn, Germany; Kunstruimte, Groningen, Netherlands
'Music for the Bionic Ear', Unsound Festival, Cracow, Poland
2010 'Proof of Concept', Centre for Contemporary Photography, Melbourne
2007 'Volta', Asian Art Biennale, Taipei, Taiwan
2006 'Volta', RoslynOxley9, Sydney; Orange Regional Art Gallery, Orange, NSW

SELECTED SOLO PERFORMANCES

2012 Mutek Festival, Montreal, Canada
MONA FOMA (Museum of Old and New Art's Festival of Music and Art), Hobart
2011 Multiplace Festival, Bratislava, Slovakia
Unsound Festival, Cracow, Poland
Donaufestival, Krems, Austria
Elevate Festival, Graz, Austria
Trama Festival, Porto, Portugal
2010 17th Biennale of Sydney
Fri Resonans Festival, Trondheim, Norway
Mois Multi Festival, Quebec City, Canada
Vancouver New Music Festival, Vancouver, Canada
Henie-Onstad Kunstsenter, Oslo, Norway
2009 Palace of Culture and Science, Musica Genera Festival, Warsaw, Poland
2008 Yokohama Triennale, Japan

COMPOSITION AND AUDIOVISUAL DESIGN FOR DANCE

2011 Chunky Move: *Connected*, Melbourne Dance Massive; Sydney Theatre; Arko Arts Theatre, Seoul; Lincoln Hall, Portland, Arizona; Reynolds Theatre, Durham, North Carolina, Arizona; Joyce Theatre, New York; Loeb Playhouse, Lafayette, Indiana; Hatfield Hall, Terre Haute, Indiana; Zellerbach Theatre, Philadelphia; Luckman Fine Arts Complex, Los Angeles; MASS MoCa, North Adams, Massachusetts; Wesleyan University, Middletown, Connecticut, Arizona; Scottsdale Centre for Performing Arts, Phoenix; Meany Hall, Seattle; Mandeville Auditorium, San Diego
Drift, Dance Massive, Campbelltown Arts Centre, Sydney
2008 Chunky Move: *Mortal Engine*, Sydney Festival; Edinburgh Festival; Noorderzan Festival, Groningen, Netherlands; International Arts Festival, Salamanca, Spain; Tanzhaus, Germany; New Wave Festival, New York; Live Arts Festival, Philadelphia; Chiang Kai-Shek Cultural Centre, Taipei; New Vision Arts Festival, Hong Kong; Festival de Mexico, Mexico City

QUALIFICATIONS, RESIDENCIES AND AWARDS

2012 *3 Studies for the Bionic Ear*, Paris Rostrum of Composers (selection), France
2011–12 Artist in Residence, Salamanca Arts Centre, Hobart
2011 *Interior Design Music for the Bionic Ear*, Future Everything Award (short-listed), Manchester, UK
Composer in Residence, Bionic Ear Institute, Melbourne
2010 Chunky Move: *Mortal Engine* (honourable mention), Prix Ars Electronica, Austria
2009 Chunky Move: *Mortal Engine* (best visual production), Helpmann Award
2006 PhD (Music Composition), Monash University, Melbourne
2003–06 Australian Postgraduate Award (PhD), Monash University, Melbourne
2003 Master of Musicology, Monash University, Melbourne
2000–02 Monash Graduate Scholarship (MA), Monash University, Melbourne
2000 Australian Musicological Society Award (winner, Victorian chapter)
1999 Bachelor of Arts (Honours), La Trobe University, Melbourne

SELECTED BIBLIOGRAPHY

Byrne, Ben. 'Cross-generational experimentation'. *Realtime*, no.89, February–March, 2009, p.41.
Charles, Simon. 'Another acoustic reality'. *Realtime*, no.102, April–May, 2011, p.39.
Evans, Kathy. 'Sonic tonic for bionic ear'. *Age*, 21 December 2010, <http://www.theage.com.au/entertainment/music/sonic-tonic-for-bionic-ear-20101220-1932w.html#ixzz1yrVlrL9T>, viewed 27 June 2012.
Gallasch, Keith. 'A feral universe'. *Realtime*, no.83, February–March, 2008, p.15.
Gook, Ben. 'Autistic Daughters' [review]. *Mess and Noise Magazine*, 14 January 2007, <http://www.messandnoise.com/reviews/542098>, viewed 27 June 2012.
Healy, Sean. 'Pop optics' [review]. *Skynoise*, 4 December 2006, <http://www.skynoise.net/2006/12/04/pop-optics/>, viewed 27 June 2012.
Linguey, Dean. 'Making music at the interface'. *Realtime*, no.81, October–November, 2007.
Mangan, John. 'A sound idea, just like an Egyptian'. *Age*, 20 November 2011, <http://www.theage.com.au/entertainmentmusic/a-sound-idea-just-like-an-egyptian-20111119-1noma.html>, viewed 27 June 2012.
Marshall, Jonathan. 'Vertiginous pleasures of disconnection'. *Realtime*, no.79, June–July, 2007, p.40.
Mitchell, Samara, 'Better out than in', *Eyeline*, Spring, no.58, 2005.
O'Neill, Shannon. 'The sound of bicycles singing'. *Realtime*, no.90, April–May, 2009, p.48.
Plagne, Francis. *Robin Fox: Proof of Concept* [exhibition catalogue]. Centre for Contemporary Photography, Melbourne, 2010.
Priest, Gail. '3-D and other worlds'. *Realtime*, no.61, June–July, 2004, p.52.
Priest, Gail. 'Liquid Architecture 6: Celebrating sound'. *Realtime*, no.68, August–September, 2005, p.49.
Reid, Chris. 'Sound in mind and body'. *Realtime*, no.81, October–November, 2007, p.45.
Stern, Joel. 'discrete/discreet'. *Realtime*, no.79, June–July, 2007, p.36.
Stern, Joel. 'New horizons for audio-visuality'. *Realtime*, no.71, February–March, 2006, p.12.

WEBSITE

http://robinfox.net

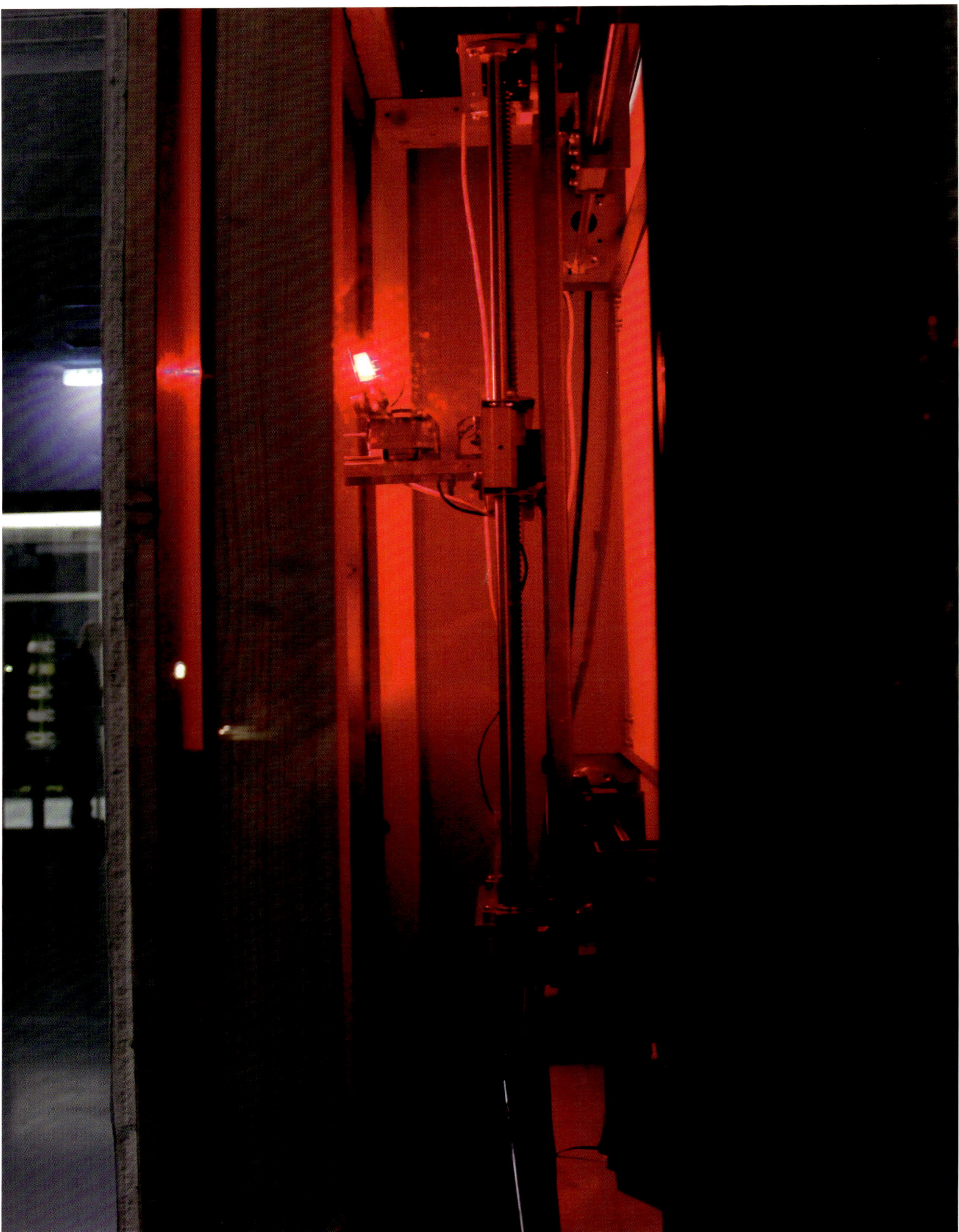

Petra Gemeinboeck

b.1971 Vienna
Lives and works in Sydney

Rob Saunders

b.1971 London
Lives and works in Sydney

Zwischenräume (installation view, detail) 2010–12
Robotics, electronics, custom artificial intelligence software, aluminium, steel, wood, plasterboard
Installed dimensions variable
Courtesy: The artists

JOINT EXHIBITIONS

2011–13	'Love Lace', Powerhouse Museum, Sydney
2011	'Politik der Wand', Forum Stadtpark, Graz, Austria
2010	'Zwischenräume', Schauraum Angewandte, MuseumsQuartier, Vienna

JOINT RESIDENCIES

2012	Artists in Residence, Ars Electronica Futurelab, Linz, Austria
2010	Artists in Residence, Digitale Kunst, University of Applied Arts, Vienna

Petra Gemeinboeck

SELECTED EXHIBITIONS

2010	'Biennale Cuvée: World Selection of Contemporary Art', OK Center for Contemporary Art, Linz, Austria
2009	'e-MobiLArt', Thessaloniki Biennale, State Museum of Contemporary Art, Thessaloniki, Greece
2006	'Intensive Science', Maison Rouge, Paris
2005	'Impossible Geographies 1.1', Fabrica Gallery, Brighton, UK
	'Presence and Absence', Institute of Contemporary Arts, Singapore
2004	'La ville à nu/The naked city: Archilab 2004', Orléans, France
	'MAK NITE', Museum of Applied Arts, Vienna
2003	'Code: The Language of our Time', Ars Electronica Festival, Ars Electronica Center, Linz, Austria
	'Pressentiments II', Centre des Arts d'Enghien-les-Bains, Paris
	'Version>03 Digital Arts Convergence', Festival of Digital Media Arts, Museum of Contemporary Art, Chicago
2001	'Takeover', Ars Electronica Festival, Ars Electronica Center, Linz, Austria
	'The Adventure of Cave', NTT InterCommunication Center, Tokyo
1996	'Labyrinth', European Capital of Culture, Copenhagen

QUALIFICATIONS, RESIDENCIES AND GRANTS

Present	Senior Lecturer, Interactive Media Arts, College of Fine Arts, UNSW, Sydney
2012	Artist in Residence, Cité Internationale des Arts, Paris
	Inter-Arts Project Grant, Australia Council for the Arts, Sydney
2010	New Work Grant, Media Arts Board, Austrian Federal Ministry for Education, the Arts and Culture, Vienna
	Inter-Arts Project Grant, Australia Council for the Arts, Sydney
	Artist in Residence, Artspace Sydney
	Artist in Residence, Bundanon Trust, NSW
2008	New Work Grant, Media Arts Board, Austrian Federal Ministry for Education, the Arts and Culture, Vienna
2006	Visiting artist, Sony Computer Science Labs (CSL), Paris
2005	Artist in Residence, DoWhile Studio New Media Art Residency, Boston
2004	Doctor of Technical Sciences in Visual Culture, Faculty of Architecture, Vienna University of Technology, Austria
2003	Master of Fine Arts (Electronic Visualization), School of Art and Design, University of Illinois, Chicago
2000	Master of Architecture, Faculty of Architecture, University of Stuttgart, Germany
1999	Visiting Artist, Fraunhofer Institute, Stuttgart, Germany

Rob Saunders

QUALIFICATIONS, GRANTS, AWARDS AND COLLABORATIONS

Present	Senior Lecturer, Design Computing, Design Lab, University of Sydney
2006	'Curious Places', Australian Research Council Discovery Project Grant DP0666584
2005	*The Difference Engine*, collaboration with James Coupe and Juan Pampin, Stills Gallery, Edinburgh, Scotland
2002	Doctor of Philosophy, University of Sydney
1995	'Interactive Evolution of Virtual Sculptures', Young Software Engineer of the Year, Scottish Software Federation (awarded 3rd prize)
1995	Howe Prize, University of Edinburgh, Scotland
	Bachelor of Science (Artificial Intelligence and Computer Science) (Honours), University of Edinburgh, Scotland

SELECTED BIBLIOGRAPHY

Dewdney, Andrew and Ride, Peter. 'Programming for design: Rob Saunders'. In *The New Media Handbook*. Routledge, New York, 2006.

Hötzl, Manuela. 'Petra Gemeinboeck's architektonischer aktivismus'. *Architekturtheorie Magazin*, 2010, see <http://www.architekturtheorie.eu >.

Hötzl, Manuela. 'Whirl room: Petra Gemeinboeck's CAVE installation at Ars Electronica'. *Spike Art Quarterly*, vol.1, no.1, 2004.

Kihm, Christophe. 'Extensions, derivations'. In *Intensive Science*. Sony Computer Science Laboratory, Paris, 2005.

McQuaid, Cate. 'Interactive work evokes complex memories'. *Boston Globe*, 12 August 2005.

McQuaid, Cate. 'Year brought prolific creativity, cultivated and raw'. *Boston Globe*, 30 December 2005.

Munster, Anna. 'The thought provoking jolt: Anna Munster explores Petra Gemeinboeck's impossible geographies'. *Realtime*, no.82, December–January, 2007–08, p.28.

Robertson, Barbara. 'Immersed in art'. *Computer Graphics World*, vol.11, no.1, 2001.

Ward, Lindie. 'Openwork patterns'. *Artlink*, vol.32, no.1, 2012.

WEBSITES

www.impossiblegeographies.net
www.robococo.net

This work was supported by a 2010 New Work Grant from the Media Arts Board, Austrian Federal Ministry for Education, the Arts and Culture. Underlying research was supported under the Australian Research Council's Discovery Projects funding scheme (project number DP0666584). Engineering consultants: Icy Labs; fabrication support: Marjo Niemela and ATSC, University of Sydney.

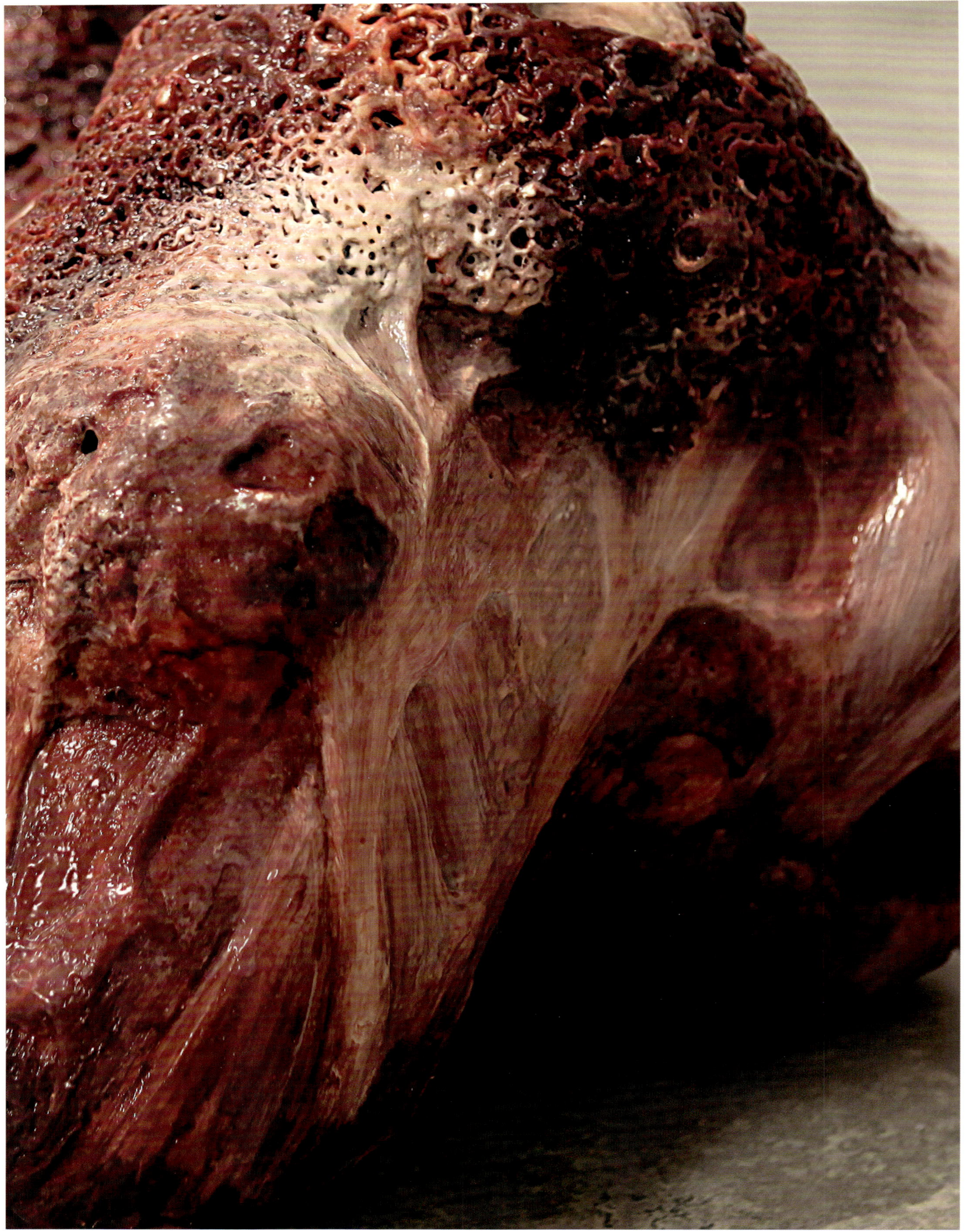

Ian Haig

b.1964 Melbourne
Lives and works in Melbourne

Some Thing (detail) 2011
Production and fabrication: Fiona Edwards; robotics and electronics: Martin James; sound: PH2 (Philip Brophy and Philip Samartzis)
Robotics, electronics, latex, surround sound (loop)
40 x 40 x 120cm (irreg.)
Funded with the assistance of the Australia Council Inter-Arts Office 2011

SOLO EXHIBITIONS

2011 'Tyger, Tyger' (with Kotoe Ishii), West Space Gallery, Melbourne
'Chronicles of the New Human Organism', Centre for Contemporary Photography, Melbourne
2010 'Chronicles of the New Human Organism', Institute of Modern Art, Brisbane
2007 'Zoso' (with Philip Samartzis and DarrenTofts), Project Space Gallery, RMIT, Melbourne
2006 'The Dirt Factory', Victorian College of the Arts Gallery, Melbourne
'Sick', Conical Gallery, Melbourne
2005 'Flesh Coloured Plastic', Esa Jaske Gallery, Sydney
'Flesh Coloured Plastic', Spacement Gallery, Melbourne
'The Dirt Factory', Experimental Art Foundation, Adelaide
'Bimbo Laboratory', CAST Gallery, Hobart
2004 'Futurotica', Erotica LA, Los Angeles
2003 'Futurotica', Sexpo, Melbourne
'Human Aquatic Breeding Centre', Perth Institute of Contemporary Art, Perth
'Premonition' (with Martine Corompt and Chris Langton), Span Gallery, Melbourne
'My Favourite Babe', Canberra Contemporary Art Space, Canberra
2002 'Brain Tumour Helmets with Microwaves', Centre for Contemporary Photography, Melbourne
2001 'Anti Ergonomic Hump Machine', West Space Gallery, Melbourne
2000 'Colossus: Super Human Factory Online Project Sex Computer 2000 Unit', First Floor Gallery, Melbourne
1997 'Trick or Treat' (with Martine Corompt and Philip Samartzis), 200 Gertrude Street, Melbourne
1992 'The Thing with 200 Heads', Paper Heroes Gallery, Melbourne

SELECTED GROUP EXHIBITIONS

2011 'Southern Panoramas', 17th International Contemporary Art Festival, Videobrasil, São Paulo, Brazil
'Awfully Wonderful', Performance Space, Sydney
2010 'New Media, Sex, and Culture in the 21st Century', Museum of New Art, Detroit
2009 'The Shilo Project', Ian Potter Museum of Art, Melbourne, and regional tour
2008 'The Bon Scott Project', Fremantle Arts Centre, Perth
2006 'Eyes, Lies and Illusions', Australian Centre for the Moving Image, Melbourne
2003 'Odd', Faculty Gallery, Royal Melbourne Institute of Technology, Melbourne
2002 'Moist', Multimedia Art Asia Pacific Festival, Art Museum of China, Beijing
'Peepshow 28', Lusty Lady adult cinema complex, San Francisco and Seattle
'Arte Red', ARCO, Madrid
2001 'Waste', Experimenta Media Arts, Melbourne Festival for the Arts, Blackbox, Melbourne
'Sticky Fingers', Para/Site Gallery, Hong Kong
2000 'The 2nd International City Video Installation – Akihabara TV', Tokyo
1999 'National Digital Art Awards', Institute of Modern Art, Brisbane
1995 'The 4th International Biennale', ARTEC 95, Nagoya, Japan
'The Sixth International Symposium on Electronic Art', Montreal, Canada
'Virtualalities', Scienceworks, Melbourne
1992 'The Third International Symposium on Electronic Art', Museum of Contemporary Art, Sydney
1991 'Association City', 200 Gertrude Street, Melbourne

SELECTED QUALIFICATIONS, RESIDENCIES, GRANTS AND AWARDS

2011 Australia Council for the Arts Inter-Arts Office Grant
2010 PhD (in progress), College of Fine Arts, UNSW, Sydney
2008 Artist in Residence, Australia Council for the Arts, Visual Arts Board, Studio Residency, Los Angeles
2006 Artist in Residence, Asialink Studio Residency, Ssamzie Space, Seoul
2002 Fellowship, New Media Arts Board, Australia Council for the Arts, Sydney (2003–2004)
Masstерraton (with Martine Corompt), Victoria Commissions, Arts Victoria, in association with the State Library of Victoria, Experimedia Courtyard
2001 Digital Media Fund (with Martine Corompt and Chris Langton), Cinemedia, Melbourne
1999 Artist in Residence, Australia Council for the Arts, Visual Arts Board, Studio Residency, Tokyo
1997–98 Master's Degree, Media Arts, Department of Visual Communication, RMIT, Melbourne
1993 Film Development/Production Investment Grant, Australian Film Commission
1990 Graduate Diploma of Art, Phillip Institute of Technology (now RMIT), Melbourne

SELECTED BIBLIOGRAPHY

Colless, Edward. 'Freak'. In *Human Aquatic Breeding Centre* [exhibition catalogue]. Perth Institute of Contemporary Art, Perth, 2003.
Cook, Robert. 'The Bon Scott Project', *Art Monthly Australia*, no.216, 2008.
Crawford, Ashley. 'Flesh Coloured Plastic' [preview]. *Australian Art Collector*, no.31, January–March, 2005.
Crawford, Ashley. 'The Dirt Factory' [preview]. *Sunday Age*, 30 April 2006.
Feldman, Allen. 'The digital miniature: Private perceptions in a public space'. In *Under_Score* [exhibition catalogue]. Next Wave Festival, Brooklyn Academy of Music (BAM), New York, 2001
Fliedner, Kelly. *Tyger, Tyger* [exhibition catalogue]. West Space Gallery, Melbourne, 2011.
Mitchell, Samara. 'Better out than in', *Eyeline*, Spring, no.58, 2005.
Palmer, Daniel. 'Wilful waste'. *Realtime*, no.46, December–January, 2001–02.
Rossiter, Ned. 'Web devolution: Working the screen', *Realtime*, no. 45, October–November, 2001.
Stuckey, Helen. 'Art at the crossroads', *Realtime*, no.82, December–January, 2007.
Stuckey, Helen. *Nothing Natural* [exhibition catalogue]. Basement Gallery, Melbourne, 1997.
Tofts, Darren. 'Hexadecimal Dump.exe: Floating thoughts on toilets, media and technology'. In *Excelsior 3000: Bowel Technology Project* [exhibition catalogue]. Experimenta Media Arts, Melbourne, 2001.
Tofts, Darren. 'K-Rad Man: The reanimation of Ian Haig', *Mesh*, no.14, 2000.
Tofts, Darren. 'Transition aborted', *Photofile*, no.90, 2010.

COLLECTIONS

National Library of Australia Film and Video Lending Collection
Australian Centre for the Moving Image, Melbourne
Griffith Artworks, Queensland
Ssamzie Space, Seoul
Australian Video Art Archive, Monash University, Victoria
Private collections

WEBSITE

www.ianhaig.net

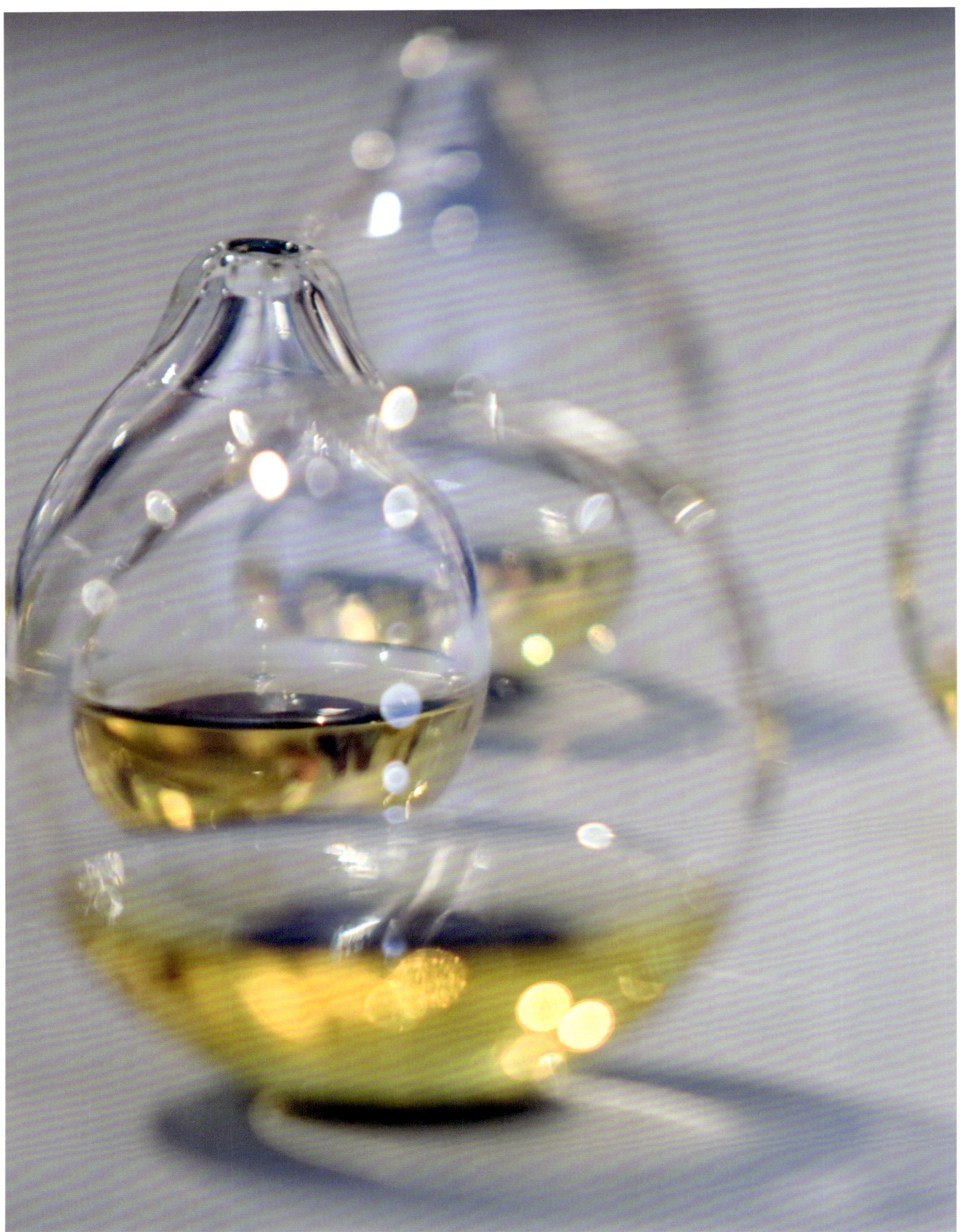

Leah Heiss

b.1973 Darwin
Lives and works in Melbourne

Polarise (detail) 2009
Magnetic liquid, propylene glycol, ethanol, glass vessels, motors, rare earth magnets, table
7 vessels: 5 x 5cm (each, irreg.)
Photograph: Narelle Sheean
Courtesy: The artist

SELECTED SOLO EXHIBITIONS

2009	'levitas', fortyfivedownstairs, Melbourne
2008	'liminal', RMIT Gallery, Melbourne
2006	'Empathy and the Space Between', Brightspace Gallery, Melbourne
2005	'Elastic Field', West Space Gallery, Melbourne

SELECTED GROUP EXHIBITIONS

2012	'Embracing Innovation', Craft ACT, Canberra
2011	'genart_sys: a window on digital culture', Australia Council for the Arts, Sydney
2010	'Signs of Change', Midland Atelier, Perth
2009	'Super Human', RMIT Gallery, Melbourne
	'showing off', Bathurst Regional Gallery, Bathurst, NSW
	'Convergence', Yarra Lane, Melbourne
2008	'In.tangible.scape.s', CWF, Antwerp, Belgium
	'Refashioning the Fashion', Object Gallery, Sydney
	'FUSE', Jam Factory, Adelaide
2007	'Strangely Familiar', SASA Gallery, Adelaide
	'Wear Now Shopfront Exhibition', High Tea with Mrs Woo, Electrofringe Festival, Newcastle, NSW
2005	'Wearable Futures', University of Wales, Newport, UK
2004	'Architecture Biennale Beijing', UHN Global Village, Beijing
	'(IM)Material', First Site Gallery, Melbourne

QUALIFICATIONS, RESIDENCIES AND GRANTS

2008	Australia Council for the Arts Visual Arts Grant
2007	Arts Victoria AIR Residency, with Nanotechnology Victoria and Australian Network for Art and Technology (ANAT)
2004–06	Master of Design (Spatial Information Architecture Laboratory), RMIT University, Melbourne
1999–02	Bachelor of Arts (Interior Design) (First Class Honours), RMIT University, Melbourne
1991–93	Bachelor of Arts (Communications), University of Canberra

SELECTED BIBLIOGRAPHY

ABC Radio Australia. 'Jewellery to deliver medicine' [radio interview], *Innovations*, 3 August 2009, <http://www.radioaustralia.net.au/international/radio/onairhighlights/jewellery-to-deliver-medicine>, viewed 12 June 2012.

ABC Radio National. 'Trends and products: Jewellery and medicine' [radio interview], *By Design*, 5 November 2008, <http://www.abc.net.au/radionational/programs/bydesign/trends-and-products-jewellery-and-medicine/3177214>, viewed 12 June 2012.

ABC Television. 'Designing the future: Medical jewellery [television interview]', *The New Inventors*, November 2008, <http://www.abc.net.au/tv/newinventors/txt/s2416729.htm>, viewed 12 June 2012.

Cauchi, Stephen. 'Drug dispensing jewellery'. *Age*, 7 December 2008.

Edgar, Ray. 'Intimate scale', *Age*, 18 March 2009.

Freeman-Greene, Suzy. 'Band of hope', *Age*, 3 November 2007. <http://www.theage.com.au/news/arts/band-of-hope/2007/11/02/1193619117811.html?page=fullpage>, viewed 12 June 2012.

O'Dwyer, Erin. 'Ring of life', *Sydney Morning Herald*, 25 August 2008. <http://www.smh.com.au/news/innovations/ring-of-life/2008/08/25/1219516362612.html>, viewed 12 June 2012.

Pomazan, Liliana. 'Fashion frontiers'. In English, Bonnie and Pomazan, Liliana (eds). *Australian Fashion Unstitched: The Last 60 Years*. Cambridge University Press, Port Melbourne, Victoria, 2010, pp.276–88.

Siggia, Stefano. 'Touching the intangible', *Flanders Today*, 26 November 2008.

Smith, Tanalee. 'Australian designer blends art, science, fashion', *Taiwan News*, 15 May 2009, <http://www.etaiwannews.com/etn/news_content php?id=949567&lang=eng_news&cate_img=317.jpg&cate_rss=news_Features>, viewed 12 June 2012.

WEBSITE

www.elasticfield.com

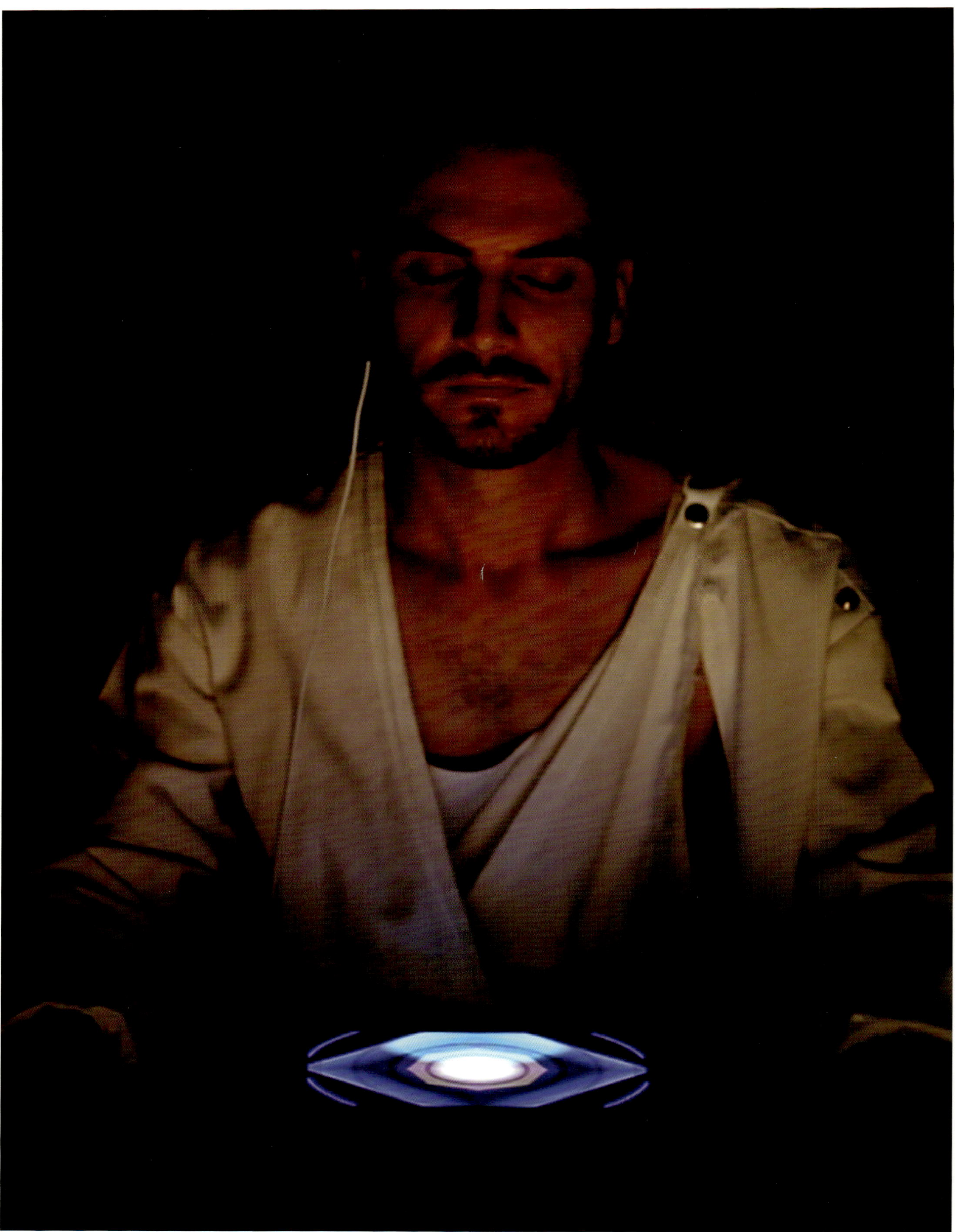

George Poonkhin Khut

b.1969 Adelaide
Lives and works in Sydney

Distillery: Waveforming (Portrait of Rob, January 2012) (still, detail) 2012
Camera: Julia Pendrill Charles; styling: Troy Brennan
HD video: colour, stereo, 12 mins
Courtesy: The artist

SELECTED SOLO EXHIBITIONS

2011	'BrightHearts: Prototypes and Preliminary Research', DABLAB Gallery, University of Technology, Sydney
2010	'Thinking through the Body: Wii-Leaf' (collaboration with Jonathan Duckworth, Lizzie Muller, Catherine Truman, Maggie Slattery, Garth Paine, Lian Loke and Somaya Langley), DABLAB Gallery, University of Technology, Sydney
2009	'The Heart Library Project', St Vincent's Public Hospital, Sydney
2002	'Nightshift' (with Wendy McPhee), Artspace, Sydney; Tasmanian Museum and Art Gallery, Hobart
2001	'Chinoiseries' Gallery 4A, Asia Australia Arts Centre, Sydney
2000	'Pillow Songs', 24HR ART, Darwin
1999	'Pillow Songs' Gallery 4A, Sydney

SELECTED GROUP EXHIBITIONS

2012	'Wonderland: New Contemporary Art from Australia', Museum of Contemporary Art, Taipei, Taiwan
2009	Inaugural exhibition, Royal Institution of Australia, Adelaide
	'Super Human', Australian Network for Art and Technology, RMIT Gallery, Melbourne
	'Peripheral', Project Space, RMIT Gallery, Melbourne
2008	'Enfoldings & Disclosures' (with Lisa Jones), University of Technology Sydney Gallery, Sydney
	'Mirror States', Campbelltown Arts Centre, New South Wales; Moving Image Centre, Auckland, NZ
2007	'I Took a Deep Breath', Biennale of Electronic Arts Perth, Perth Institute of Contemporary Art, Perth
2006	'Strange Attractors', Zendai Museum of Modern Art, Shanghai, China
	'This Secret Location', Inbetween Time Festival of Live Art and Intrigue, Arnolfini, Bristol, UK
2005	'Open Letter: Phase Two', Gallery 4A, Sydney; Metropolitan Museum of Modern Art, Manila, The Philippines; National Art Gallery, Bangkok, Thailand
	'Cardiomorphologies v.2' (with Lizzie Muller and Greg Turner), Beta_space, Powerhouse Museum, Sydney
2004	'Asian Traffic: Phase Four', Gallery 4A, Sydney
2003	'Inbetween Time 2003' (with Wendy McPhee), Arnolfini, Bristol, UK
1996	'Mutiny on the Docks,' Hobart Summer Festival, Customs House, Tasmanian Museum and Art Gallery, Hobart

QUALIFICATIONS, RESIDENCIES, GRANTS AND AWARDS

2011	Artist in Residence, collaboration with Dr Angie Morrow, Kids', Rehab Unit, Children's Hospital at Westmead, NSW
	Research Associate, Interaction Design and Human Practices (IDHuP) Lab, University of Technology, Sydney
	Speechless, Luscious Apparatus creative development residency, Critical Path, Sydney, with Lian Loke, Tess De Quincy, Justin Shoulder and Baki Kokaballi Studio residency, Queen Street Studios, Fraser Studio, Sydney
2009	Research Group Residency, 'Thinking through the Body' (ArtLab '08, Australia Council for the Arts), Bundanon, NSW
2008	Interdisciplinary Research Project 'Thinking through the Body' (ArtLab '08, Australia Council for the Arts), with Lizzie Muller, Catherine Truman, Jonathan Duckworth, Garth Paine, Maggie Slattery, Lian Loke and Somaya Langley
2006	Doctorate of Creative Arts (Research), University of Western Sydney, NSW
2004	Headspace Artist Residency, Performance Space, Sydney
1993	Bachelor of Fine Arts (Sculpture), University of Tasmania, Hobart

SELECTED BIBLIOGRAPHY

Jaspers, Anneke. 'The heart library'. In Cleland, Kathy and Muller, Lizzie (eds). *Mirror States*. Campbelltown City Art Gallery, NSW, and MIC Toi Rerehiko, Auckland, 2006.

McDowell, David. 'Body doubles: Kinesthetics and visual display in the aesthetics of gallery-based interactive art'. *EXTENSIONS: The Online Journal of Embodiment and Technology*, vol.3, 2006, <http://www.performancestudies.ucla.edu/extensionsjournal/mcdowell.htm>.

Muller, Lizzie. 'It's all about you'. In Ivanova, Antoanetta (ed.). *Strange Attractors: Charm between Art and Science*. Novamedia, Melbourne, 2006.

Veel, Kristin. 'Calm imaging: The conquest of overload and the conditions of attention'. In Ekman, Ulrik (ed.). *Throughout: Art and Culture Emerging with Ubiquitous Computing*. MIT Press, Cambridge, Massachusetts, 2012.

WEBSITES

http://georgekhut.com/
http://thinkingthroughthebody.net/

This work was supported by the Australian Network for Art and Technology and the Kids' Rehab Unit, Children's Hospital at Westmead, in association with the Australian Government through the Australia Council for the Arts, its arts funding and advisory body. Photography and video: Julia Pendrill Charles; styling: Troy Brennan; signal analysis software: Angelo Fraietta (Smart Controller) and Tuan M Vu; iOS visual effects software: Jason McDermott (ARUP Informatics), adapted from original code by Greg Turner. Special thanks to: Dr Angie Morrow (Kids' Rehab Unit), Frank Maguire (electronics and design) and Kevin Jackson.

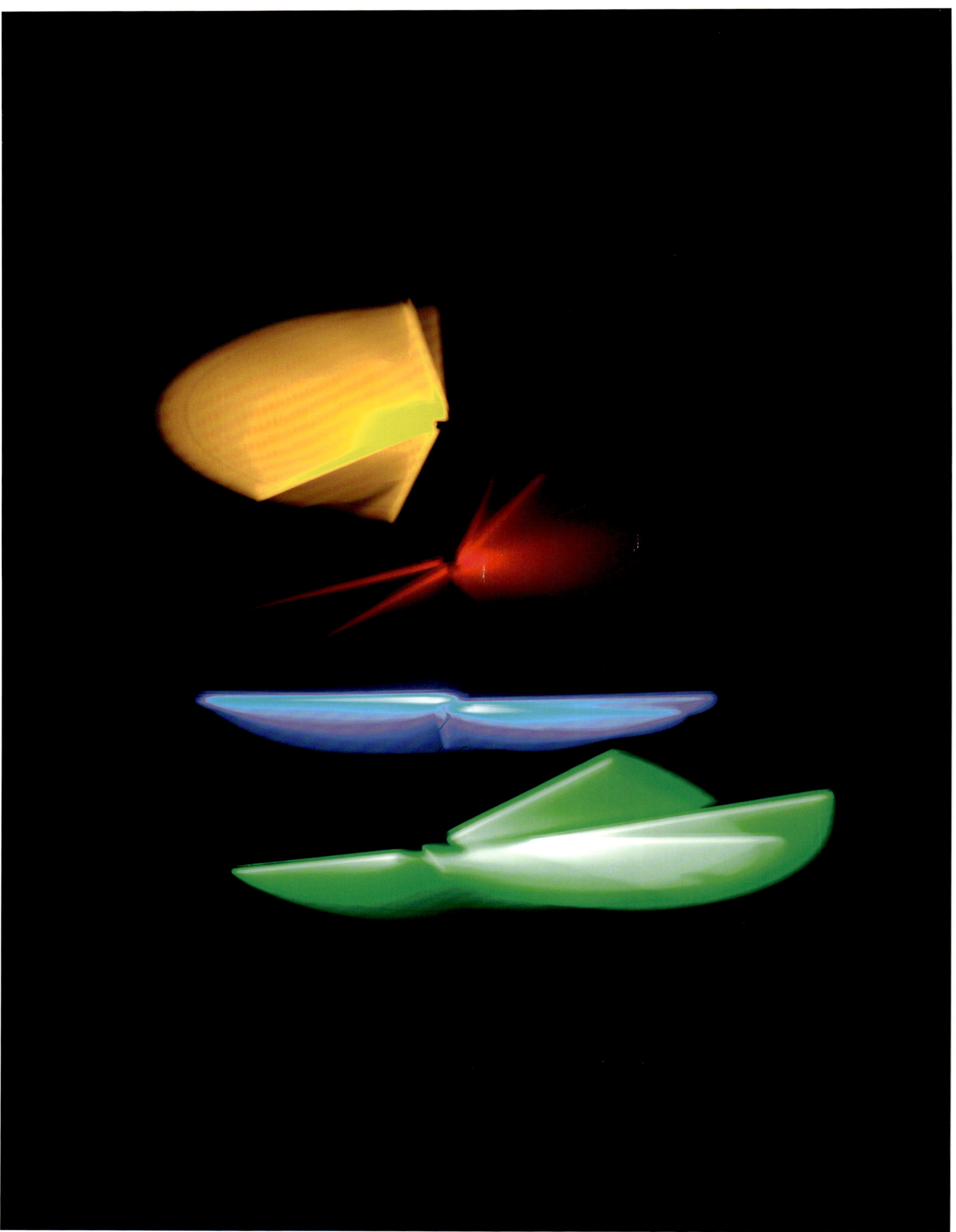

Ross Manning

b.1978 Brisbane
Lives and works in Brisbane

Spectra I (installation view) 2012
Coloured fluorescent lamps, motorised fans, power boards, extension cables, wood, rope
Installed dimensions variable
Collection: Monash University Museum of Art, Melbourne

SOLO EXHIBITIONS

2012 'Spectra', Milani Gallery, Brisbane
2011 'Gleaning the Cube', Milani Gallery, Brisbane
2010 '3 songs', Long Gallery, Salamanca Arts Centre, Museum of Old and New Art Festival of Music and Art, Hobart
'Double Refraction', Lismore Regional Gallery, NSW
2009 'Input Ruins', Milani Gallery, Brisbane
'Sunshine and Zincaloom', Ptarmigan Electronic Art Space, Helsinki

GROUP EXHIBITIONS

2012 'NEW12', Australian Centre for Contemporary Art, Melbourne
'Tetsuya Umeda and Ross Manning', KickArts Contemporary Arts, Cairns
2011 'The Festival of New Primitive', SPEC, Brisbane
'The Plastic Arts', Wandering Room, Brisbane
'Ruckus', Wandering Room, Brisbane
'Out Hear', Footscray Art Centre, Melbourne
'New Psychedelia', University of Queensland Art Museum, Brisbane
2009 'Come Hither Noise', Fremantle Arts Centre, Fremantle, WA
'Primavera '09', Museum of Contemporary Art, Sydney
'The New Truth to Materials', Boxcopy Gallery, Brisbane
'The Light', Milani Gallery, Brisbane
'Batteries Not Included', Australian Centre for Photography, Sydney
2008 'The New Fresh Cut', Institute of Modern Art, Brisbane
2006 'Lost Garden Found', Nextwave Festival, Melbourne
2003 'Take Me to Your Ruler', The Farm, Brisbane

PERFORMANCES

2007 Electrofringe Festival, Newcastle, NSW
Audio Pollen Social Club [performance], Brisbane
Sound Crucible', Ballina, NSW
2006 Liquid Architecture Festival of Sound Arts, Brisbane and Melbourne
Articulating space [performance], ABC Radio
2005 What Is Music? Festival, Melbourne
Straight Out of Brisbane Festival, Brisbane
The NOW now Festival, Sydney
2004 Electrofringe Festival, Newcastle, NSW
2003 *Small black box* [performance], Institute of Modern Art, Brisbane
Make it now [performance], Institute of Modern Art, Brisbane

QUALIFICATIONS, RESIDENCIES, GRANTS AND AWARDS

2011 'The Churchie National Emerging Art Exhibition', Griffith University Art Gallery, Brisbane (winner)
Artist Residency, Footscray Community Art Centre, Melbourne
2009 Aphids 'Choose Your Own Adventure' Residency and Mentoring, Helsinki
Artist Residency, Koelse Experimental Music Association, Helsinki
Artist Residency, Ptarmigan Electronic Art Space, Helsinki

COLLECTIONS

Museum of Contemporary Art, Sydney
Museum of Old and New Art, Hobart
University of Queensland Art Museum, Brisbane
Monash University Museum of Art, Melbourne

BIBLIOGRAPHY

Bridgeman, Sean. 'Musicians and boffins, tinkers and dreamers'. In Priest, Gail (ed.). *Experimental Music: Audio Explorations in Australia*. University of New South Wales Press, Sydney, 2008, pp.175–95.

Gomes, Mark. 'New everyday automata'. In Kahn, Jeff (ed.). *Primavera '09* [exhibition catalogue]. Museum of Contemporary Art, Sydney, 2009, p.52.

Moody, Sebastian. *New Psychedelia* [exhibition catalogue]. University of Queensland Art Museum, Brisbane, 2011.

Werkmeister, Sarah. *Double Refraction* [exhibition catalogue]. Lismore Regional Gallery, Lismore, New South Wales, 2010.

Zuvela, Dani. 'Ross Manning's *Spectra*'. In Kahn, Jeff and Engberg, Juliana (eds). *NEW12* [exhibition catalogue]. Australian Centre for Contemporary Art, Melbourne, 2012, pp.16–23.

Zuvela, Dani. 'Spectra'. In *Spectra* [exhibition catalogue]. Milani Gallery, Brisbane, 2012, unpaginated.

WEBSITES

www.rossmanning.com
www.milanigallery.com.au
www.skyneedle.org

THE 'NATIONAL NEW MEDIA ART AWARD 2012' SELECTION COMMITTEE

Suhanya Raffel, Deputy Director, Curatorial and Collection Development, QAGOMA
Daniel Crooks, new media artist
Amy Barrett-Lennard, Director, Perth Institute of Contemporary Arts

The Queensland Art Gallery | Gallery of Modern Art gratefully acknowledges the artists, selection committee and the individuals and organisations who assisted with this project. The curators met with numerous artists and curators around the country during their research for the Award, and would like to extend their sincere gratitude to everyone who was generous with their time. Particular thanks go to Oran Catts, Anna Davis, Bec Dean, Michael Edwards, Noel Frankham, Mark Feary, Blair French, Kylie Johnson, Helen Hyatt-Johnston, Jeff Kahn, Emma McRae, Abigail Moncrieff, Leigh Robb and Jasmin Stephens for their assistance.

QUEENSLAND ART GALLERY | GALLERY OF MODERN ART BOARD OF TRUSTEES

EXECUTIVE MANAGEMENT TEAM

Tony Ellwood, Director (until 23 July 2012)
Andrew Clark, Deputy Director, Programming and Corporate Services (until 25 July 2012)
Suhanya Raffel, Deputy Director, Curatorial and Collection Development
Celestine Doyle, Executive Manager, Marketing and Business Development

CURATORS

Peter McKay, Curator, Contemporary Australian Art
Amanda Slack-Smith, Assistant Curator, Australian Cinémathèque

EXHIBITION PROJECT TEAM

Helen Bovey, A/Head, Access, Education and Regional Services, and staff

Allan Brand, Head of Technology, and staff

Tarragh Cunningham, Exhibitions Manager, and staff

Andrew Dudley, Head of Registration
Desley Bischoff, Registrar, Exhibitions and Loans
Emma Schmeider, Registration Assistant, Exhibitions and Loans, and staff

Don Heron, Design Manager
Michael O'Sullivan, Senior Exhibition Designer
John Francia, Exhibitions Project Officer, and staff

Bronwyn Klepp, Principal Marketing and Advertising Officer
Kendall Battley, Senior Media Officer
Sarah Stratton, Senior Communication Officer, and staff

Donna McColm, Head, Public Programs, Children's Art Centre and Membership, and staff

Amanda Pagliarino, Head of Conservation, and staff

AUTHORS

Ellie Buttrose, Curatorial Assistant, Exhibitions and Research
Zoe De Luca, Curatorial Assistant, Exhibitions and Research
Bruce McLean, Curator, Indigenous Australian Art
Peter McKay, Curator, Contemporary Australian Art
Tarun Nagesh, Assistant Curator, Asian Art
Amanda Slack-Smith, Assistant Curator, Australian Cinémathèque

PUBLICATION

Tony Ellwood, Director
Suhanya Raffel, Deputy Director, Curatorial and Collection Development
Judy Gunning, Information and Publishing Services Manager
Don Heron, Design Manager
Peter McKay, Curator, Contemporary Australian Art
Amanda Slack-Smith, Assistant Curator, Australian Cinémathèque

Rebecca Mutch, Editor
Stephanie Kennard, Assistant Editor
Sally Nall, Graphic Designer

Image archive: Mark Sherwood, Assistant Photographer

Research assistance provided by the Queensland Art Gallery Research Library.